NEW SELECTED POEMS OF

Stevie Smith

3-03
4-03

A NEW DIRECTIONS BOOK

New Selected Poems contains a more generous number and representative choice than the original *Selected Poems* (chosen by the poet herself) which introduced Stevie Smith to America in 1964. The poems are arranged chronologically from 1937–1972. We would like to thank James MacGibbon, Stevie Smith's literary executor and editor of the *Collected Poems*, who has approved this selection made by Griselda Ohannessian.—The Publishers

Manufactured in the United States of America
New Directions Books are printed on acid-free paper
First published clothbound and as New Directions Paperbook 659
in 1988

Library of Congress Cataloging-in-Publication Data
Smith, Stevie, 1902–1971.
The new selected poems of Stevie Smith.
Includes index.   I. Title.
PR6037.M43A6   1988   821'.912   88-1428
ISBN 0-8112-1067-7
ISBN 0-8112-1068-5 (New Directions paperbook : pbk.)

New Directions Books are published for James Laughlin
by New Directions Publishing Corporation,
80 Eighth Avenue, New York 10011

FOURTH PRINTING

Contents

NEW SELECTED POEMS OF

Stevie Smith

On the Death
of a
German Philosopher

He wrote *The I and the It*
He wrote *The It and the Me*
He died at Marienbad
And now we are all at sea.

Papa Love Baby

My mother was a romantic girl
So she had to marry a man with his hair in curl
Who subsequently became my unrespected papa,
But that was a long time ago now.

What folly it is that daughters are always supposed to be
In love with papa. It wasn't the case with me
I couldn't take to him at all
But he took to me
What a sad fate to befall
A child of three.

I sat upright in my baby carriage
And wished mama hadn't made such a foolish marriage.
I tried to hide it, but it showed in my eyes unfortunately
And a fortnight later papa ran away to sea.

He used to come home on leave
It was always the same
I could not grieve
But I think I was somewhat to blame.

I

Egocentric

What care I if good God be
If he be not good to me,
If he will not hear my cry
Nor heed my melancholy midnight sigh?
What care I if he created Lamb,
And golden Lion, and mud-delighting Clam,
And Tiger stepping out on padded toe,
And the fecund earth the Blindworms know?
He made the Sun, the Moon and every Star,
He made the infant Owl and the Baboon,
He made the ruby-orbed Pelican,
He made all silent inhumanity,
Nescient and quiescent to his will,
Unquickened by the questing conscious flame
That is my glory and my bitter bane.
What care I if Skies are blue,
If God created Gnat and Gnu,
What care I if good God be
If he be not good to me?

Forgive me, forgive me

Forgive me forgive me my heart is my own
And not to be given for any man's frown
Yet would I not keep it for ever alone.

Forgive me forgive me I thought that I loved
My fancy betrayed me my heart was unmoved
My fancy too often has carelessly roved.

Forgive me forgive me for here where I stand
There is no friend beside me no lover at hand
No footstep but mine in my desert of sand.

Progression

I fell in love with Major Spruce
And never gave a sign
The sweetest major in the force
And only 39.

  It *is* Major Spruce
  And he's grown such a bore, such a bore,
  I used to think I was in love with him
  Well, I don't think so any more.

    It *was* the Major Spruce.
    He died. Didn't I tell you?
    He was the last of the Spruces,
    And about time too.

The Suburban Classes

There is far too much of the suburban classes
Spiritually not geographically speaking. They're asses.
Menacing the greatness of our beloved England, they lie
Propagating their kind in an eightroomed stye.
Now I have a plan which I will enfold
(There's this to be said for them, they do as they're told)
Then tell them their country's in mortal peril
They believed it before and again will not cavil
Put it in caption form firm and slick
If they see it in print it is bound to stick:
'Your King and your Country need you Dead'
You see the idea? Well, let it spread.
Have a suitable drug under string and label
Free for every Registered Reader's table.
For the rest of the gang who are not patriotic
I've another appeal they'll discover hypnotic:
Tell them it's smart to be dead and won't hurt
And they'll gobble up drug as they gobble up dirt.

Spanish School

The painters of Spain
Dipped their brushes in pain
By grief on a gallipot
Was Spanish tint begot.

Just see how Theotocopoulos
Throws on his canvas
Colours of hell
Christ lifts his head to cry

4

Once more I bleed and die
Mary emaciated cries:
Are men not satiated?
Must the blood of my son
For ever run?
The sky turns to burning oil
Blood red and yellow boil
Down from on high
Will no hills fall on us
To hide that sky?
Y Luciente's pen
Traces the life of men
Christs crucified upon a slope
They have no hope
Like Calderon who wrote in grief and scorn:
The greatest crime of man's to have been born.
Dr Péral
In a coat of gray
Has a way
With his mouth which seems to say
A lot
But nothing very good to hear
And as for Doña Ysabel Corbos de Porcel
Well
What a bitch
This seems to me a portrait which
Might have been left unhung
Or at anyrate slung
A little higher up.

But never mind there's always Ribera
With his little lamb
(Number two-four-four)
To give a more
Genial atmosphere
And a little jam
For the pill –
But still.

Up and Down

Up and down the streets they go
Tapping tapping to and fro
What they see I do not know

Up and down the streets they hurry
Push and rush and jerk and worry
Full of ineffectual flurry

Up and down the streets they run
From morning to the set of sun
I shall be glad when they have done

I shall be glad when there's an end
Of all the noise that doth offend
My soul. Still Night, don cloak, descend.

From the Greek

To many men strange fates are given
Beyond remission or recall
But the worst fate of all (tra la)
's to have no fate at all (tra la).

Infant

It was a cynical babe
Lay in its mother's arms
Born two months too soon
After many alarms
Why is its mother sad
Weeping without a friend
Where is its father – say?
He tarries in Ostend.
It was a cynical babe. Reader before you condemn, pause,
It was a cynical babe. Not without cause.

Numbers

A thousand and fifty-one waves
Two hundred and thirty-one seagulls
A cliff of four hundred feet
Three miles of ploughed fields
One house
Four windows look on the waves
Four windows look on the ploughed fields
One skylight looks on the sky
In that skylight's sky is one seagull.

Nature and Free Animals

I will forgive you everything,
But what you have done to my Dogs
I will not forgive.
You have taught them the sicknesses of your mind
And the sicknesses of your body
You have taught them to be servile
To hang servilely upon your countenance
To be dependent touching and entertaining
To have rights to be wronged
And wrongs to be righted.
You have taught them to be protected by a Society.
This I will not forgive,
Saith the Lord.
Well, God, it's all very well to talk like this
And I dare say it's all very fine
And Nature and Free Animals
Are all very fine,
Well all I can say is
If you wanted it like that
You shouldn't have created me
Not that I like it very much
And now that I'm on the subject I'll say,
What with Nature and Free Animals on the one side
And you on the other,
I hardly know I'm alive.

Eng.

What has happened to the young men of Eng.?
Why are they so lovey-dovey so sad and so domesticated
So sad and so philoprogenitive
So sad and without sensuality?
They love with a ci-devant feminine affection
They see in their dreams a little home
And *kiddies*
Ah the *kiddies*
They would not mind *having* babies:
It is unkind
Of Nature to lag behind.

Death Bereaves our Common Mother
Nature Grieves for my Dead Brother

Lamb dead, dead lamb,
He was, I am,
Separation by a tense
Baulks my eyes' indifference.
Can I see the lately dead
And not bend a sympathetic head?
Can I see lamb dead as mutton
And not care a solitary button?

The Reason

My life is vile
I hate it so
I'll wait awhile
And then I'll go.

Why wait at all?
Hope springs alive,
Good may befall
I yet may thrive.

It is because I can't make up my mind
If God is good, impotent or unkind.

I Like to Play with Him

I like to play with him
He would be lovely to play with
He is so solemn sensitive conceited
He would be lovely to play with
I could pretend
Say so-and-so and so-and-so
Watch his responses
How'd he take that today
And this tomorrow,
Mood, tense, you see
I'd conjugate His Inexcellency.

Oh on that evening you were
So charming enchanting touching
Lost wounded and betrayed
Oh that should have been only the beginning.

All Things Pass

All things pass
Love and mankind is grass.

Sunt Leones

The lions who ate the Christians on the sands of the arena
By indulging native appetites played what has now been seen a
Not entirely negligible part
In consolidating at the very start
The position of the Early Christian Church.
Initiatory rites are always bloody
And the lions, it appears
From contemporary art, made a study
Of dyeing Coliseum sands a ruddy
Liturgically sacrificial hue
And if the Christians felt a little blue –
Well people being eaten often do.
Theirs was the death, and theirs the crown undying,
A state of things which must be satisfying.
My point which up to this has been obscured
Is that it was the lions who procured
By chewing up blood gristle flesh and bone
The martyrdoms on which the Church has grown.
I only write this poem because I thought it rather looked
As if the part the lions played was being overlooked.
By lions' jaws great benefits and blessings were begotten
And so our debt to Lionhood must never be forgotten.

I do not Speak

I do not ask for mercy for understanding for peace
And in these heavy days I do not ask for release
I do not ask that suffering shall cease.

I do not pray to God to let me die
To give an ear attentive to my cry
To pause in his marching and not hurry by.

I do not ask for anything I do not speak
I do not question and I do not seek
I used to in the day when I was weak.

Now I am strong and lapped in sorrow
As in a coat of magic mail and borrow
From Time today and care not for tomorrow.

Never Again

Never again will I weep
And wring my hands
And beat my head against the wall
Because
Me nolentem fata trahunt
But
When I have had enough
I will arise
And go unto my Father
And I will say to Him:
Father, I have had enough.

Freddy

Nobody knows what I feel about Freddy
I cannot make anyone understand
I love him sub specie aeternitatis
I love him out of hand.
I don't love him so much in the restaurants that's a fact
To get him hobnob with my old pub chums needs too much
    tact
He don't love them and they don't love him
In the pub lub lights they say Freddy very dim.
But get him alone on the open saltings
Where the sea licks up to the fen
He is his and my own heart's best
World without end ahem.
People who say we ought to get married ought to get smacked:
Why should we do it when we can't afford it and have
    ourselves whacked?
Thank you kind friends and relations thank *you*,
We do very well as we do.
Oh what do I care for the pub lub lights
And the friends I love so well –
There's more in the way I feel about Freddy
Than a friend can tell.
But all the same I don't care much for his meelyoo I mean
I don't anheimate mich in the ha-ha well-off suburban scene
Where men are few and hearts go tumptytum
In the tennis club lub lights poet very dumb.
But there never was a boy like Freddy
For a haystack's ivory tower of bliss
Where speaking sub specie humanitatis
Freddy and me can kiss.
Exiled from his meelyoo
Exiled from mine
There's all Tom Tiddler's time pocket
For his love and mine.

Lord Barrenstock

Lord Barrenstock and Epicene,
What's it to me that you have been
In your pursuit of interdicted joys
Seducer of a hundred little boys?

Your sins are red about your head
And many people wish you dead.

You trod the widow in the mire
Wronged the son, deceived the sire.

You put a fence about the land
And made the people's cattle graze on sand.

Ratted from many a pool and forced amalgamation
And dealt in shares which never had a stock exchange
      quotation.

Non flocci facio, I do not care
For wrongs you made the other fellow bear:
'Tis not for these unsocial acts not these
I wet my pen. I would not have you tease,
With a repentance smug and overdue
For all the things you still desire to do,
The ears of an outraged divinity:
But oh your tie is crooked and I see
Too plain you had an éclair for your tea.

It is this nonchalance about your person –
That is the root of my profound aversion.

You are too fat. In spite of stays
Your shape is painful to the polished gaze;

Your uncombed hair grows thin and daily thinner,
In fact you're far too ugly to be such a sinner.

Lord Barrenstock and Epicene, consider all that you have done
Lord Epicene and Barrenstock, yet not two Lords but one,
I think you are an object not of fear but pity
Be good, my Lord, since you can not be pretty.

This Englishwoman

This Englishwoman is so refined
She has no bosom and no behind.

Major Macroo

Major Hawkaby Cole Macroo
Chose
Very wisely
A patient Griselda of a wife with a heart of gold
That never beat for a soul but him
Himself and his slightest whim.

He left her alone for months at a time
When he had to have a change
Just had to
And his pension wouldn't stretch to a fare for two
And he didn't want it to.

And if she wept she was game and nobody knew it
And she stood at the edge of the tunnel and waved as his train
        went through it.

And because it was cheaper they lived abroad
And did he care if she might be unhappy or bored?
He did not.
He'd other things to think of – a lot.

He'd fads and he fed them fat,
And she could lump it and that was that.

He'd several boy friends
And she thought it was nice for him to have them,
And she loved him and felt that he needed her and waited
And waited and never became exasperated.

Even his room
Was dusted and kept the same,
And when friends came
They went into every room in the house but that one
Which Hawkaby wouldn't have shown.

Such men as these, such selfish cruel men
Hurting what most they love what most loves them,
Never make a mistake when it comes to choosing a woman
To cherish them and be neglected and not think it inhuman.

Tender Only to One

Tender only to one
Tender and true
The petals swing
To my fingering
Is it you, or you, or you?

Tender only to one
I do not know his name
And the friends who fall
To the petals' call
May think my love to blame.

Tender only to one
This petal holds a clue
The face it shows
But too well knows
Who I am tender to.

Tender only to one,
Last petal's latest breath
Cries out aloud
From the icy shroud
His name, his name is Death.

Parrot

The old sick green parrot
High in a dingy cage
Sick with malevolent rage
Beadily glutted his furious eye
On the old dark
Chimneys of Noel Park

Far from his jungle green
Over the seas he came
To the yellow skies, to the dripping rain,
To the night of his despair.
And the pavements of his street
Are shining beneath the lamp
With a beauty that's not for one
Born under a tropic sun.

He has croup. His feathered chest
Knows no minute of rest.
High on his perch he sits
And coughs and spits,
Waiting for death to come.
Pray heaven it wont be long.

Infelice

Walking swiftly with a dreadful duchess,
He smiled too briefly, his face was as pale as sand,
He jumped into a taxi when he saw me coming,
Leaving me alone with a private meaning,
He loves me so much, my heart is singing.
Later at the Club when I rang him in the evening
They said: Sir Rat is dining, is dining, is dining,
No Madam, he left no message, ah how his silence speaks,
He loves me too much for words, my heart is singing.
The Pullman seats are here, the tickets for Paris, I am waiting,
Presently the telephone rings, it is his valet speaking,
Sir Rat is called away, to Scotland, his constituents,
(Ah the dreadful duchess, but he loves me best)
Best pleasure to the last, my heart is singing.
One night he came, it was four in the morning,
Walking slowly upstairs, he stands beside my bed,
Dear darling, lie beside me, it is too cold to stand speaking,
He lies down beside me, his face is like the sand,
He is in a sleep of love, my heart is singing.
Sleeping softly softly, in the morning I must wake him,
And waking he murmurs, I only came to sleep.
The words are so sweetly cruel, how deeply he loves me,
I say them to myself alone, my heart is singing.
Now the sunshine strengthens, it is ten in the morning,
He is so timid in love, he only needs to know,
He is my little child, how can he come if I do not call him,
I will write and tell him everything, I take the pen and write:
I love you so much, my heart is singing.

Silence and Tears

A priestly garment, eminently suitable for conducting funeral services in inclement weather.

From a church outfitter's catalogue

The tears of the widow of the military man
Fell down to the earth as the funeral sentence ran.
Dust to dust, Oh how frightful sighed the mourners as the
    rain began.

But the grave yawned wide and took the tears and the rain,
And the poor dead man was at last free from all his pain,
Pee-wee sang the little bird upon the tree again and again.

Is it not a solemn moment when the last word is said,
And wrapped in cloak of priestly custom we dispose our dead,
And the earth falls heavy, heavy, upon the expensive coffin
    lined with lead?

And may the coffin hold his bones in peace that lies below,
And may the widow woman's tears make a good show,
And may the suitable priestly garment not let the breath of
    scandal through.

For the weather of their happening has been a little inclement,
And would people be so sympathetic if they knew how the
    story went?
Best not put it to the test. Silence and tears are convenient.

The Murderer

My true love breathed her latest breath
And I have closed her eyes in death.
It was a cold and windy day
In March, when my love went away.
She was not like other girls – rather diffident,
And that is how we had an accident.

Reversionary

The Lion dishonoured bids death come,
The worm in like hap lingers on.
The Lion dead, his pride no less,
The world inherits wormliness.

Dear Karl

Dear Karl, I send you Walt Whitman in a sixpenny book.
'How dilettante', I hear you observe, 'I hate these selections
Arbitrarily made to meet a need that is not mine and a taste
Utterly antagonistic, wholly alien, egregiously coercionary
Of individualism's, egotism's, insolence's light-fingered ⌐
    traffickings.'
Put a leash on your indignation; hold it on a tight short leash,
Muzzle it in a tough criss-cross mesh of temporization and
    impartiality.
'God, I have no such dishonourable merchandise, such tinsel
    and tawdry in my shop window.'
So you say. Then borrow or steal a muzzle to muzzle your
    indignation,
A criss-cross wire mesh of temporization and suavity, and
    with a muzzled and leashed wrath
Hanging on your tapping heels: Listen.
If I had what hypocritical poetasters crocodilely whining call
    lucre and filthy,
But man, and it takes a man to articulate the unpalatable truth,
Means of support, if I had this and a little more,
I would give you Leaves of Grass, I would send
All of Walt Whitman to you with a smile that guesses it is
More blest to give than receive.
For I, I myself, I have no Leaves of Grass
But only Walt Whitman in a sixpenny book,
Taste's, blend's, essence's, multum-in-parvo's Walt Whitman.
And now sending it to you I say:
Fare out, Karl, on an afternoon's excursion, on a sixpenny
    unexplored uncharted road,
Over sixpennyworth of tarmac, blistered by an American sun,
    over irrupted boulders,
And a hundred freakish geology's superimpositions. Fare out
    on a strange road
Between lunchtime and dinner. Bon voyage, Karl, bon voyage.

Souvenir de Monsieur Poop

I am the self-appointed guardian of English literature,
I believe tremendously in the significance of age;
I believe that a writer is wise at 50,
Ten years wiser at 60, at 70 a sage.
I believe that juniors are lively, to be encouraged with
    discretion and snubbed,
I believe also that they are bouncing, communistic, ill
    mannered and, of course, young.
But I never define what I mean by youth
Because the word undefined is more useful for general
    purposes of abuse.
I believe that literature is a school where only those who apply
    themselves diligently to their tasks acquire merit.
And only they after the passage of a good many years (see
    above).
But then I am an old fogey.
I always write more in sorrow than in anger.
I am, after all, devoted to Shakespeare, Milton,
And, coming to our own times,
Of course
Housman.
I have never been known to say a word against the
    established classics,
I am in fact devoted to the established classics.
In the service of literature I believe absolutely in the principle
    of division;
I divide into age groups and also into schools.
This is in keeping with my scholastic mind, and enables me to
    trounce
Not only youth
(Which might be thought intellectually frivolous by pedants)
    but also periodical tendencies,
To ventilate, in a word, my own political and moral
    philosophy.

(When I say that I am an old fogey, I am, of course, joking.)
English literature, as I see it, requires to be defended
By a person of integrity and essential good humour
Against the forces of fanaticism, idiosyncrasy and anarchy.
I perfectly apprehend the perilous nature of my convictions
And I am prepared to go to the stake
For Shakespeare, Milton,
And, coming to our own times,
Of course
Housman.
I cannot say more than that, can I?
And I do not deem it advisable, in the interests of the editor
        to whom I am spatially contracted,
To say less.

My Soul

In the flame of the flickering fire
The sins of my soul are few
And the thoughts in my head are the thoughts of a bed
With a solitary view.
But the eye of eternal consciousness
Must blink as a bat blinks bright
Or ever the thoughts in my head be stilled
On the brink of eternal night.

Oh feed to the golden fish his egg
Where he floats in his captive bowl,
To the cat his kind from the womb born blind,
And to the Lord my soul.

In My Dreams

In my dreams I am always saying goodbye and riding away,
Whither and why I know not nor do I care.
And the parting is sweet and the parting over is sweeter,
And sweetest of all is the night and the rushing air.

In my dreams they are always waving their hands and saying
    goodbye,
And they give me the stirrup cup and I smile as I drink,
I am glad the journey is set, I am glad I am going,
I am glad, I am glad, that my friends don't know what I think.

Nourish Me on an Egg

Nourish me on an egg, Nanny,
And ply with bottled stout,
And I'll grow to be a man
Before the secret's out.

Nourish me on an egg, Nanny,
With bottled stout to drink,
And I'll grow to be a man
Before you can think.

Nourish me on an egg, Nanny,
Don't wring your hands and weep,
Bring me a glass of stout
And close my eyes in sleep.

Dear Muse

Dear Muse, the happy hours we have spent together.
I love you so much in wet or fine weather.
I only wish sometimes you would speak louder,
But perhaps you will do so when you are prouder.
I often think that this will be the next instant,
Meanwhile I am your most obliging confidante.

The Lads of the Village

The lads of the village, we read in the lay,
By medalled commanders are muddled away,
And the picture that the poet makes is not very gay.

Poet, let the red blood flow, it makes the pattern better,
And let the tears flow, too, and grief stand that is their begetter,
And let man have his self-forged chain and hug every fetter.

For without the juxtaposition of muddles, medals and clay,
Would the picture be so very much more gay,
Would it not be a frivolous dance upon a summer's day?

Oh sing no more: Away with the folly of commanders.
This will not make a better song upon the field of Flanders,
Or upon any field of experience where pain makes patterns
    the poet slanders.

Little Boy Sick

I am not God's little lamb
I am God's sick tiger.
And I prowl about at night
And what most I love I bite,
And upon the jungle grass I slink,
Snuff the aroma of my mental stink,
Taste the salt tang of tears upon the brink
Of my uncomfortable muzzle.
My tail my beautiful, my lovely tail,
Is warped.
My stripes are matted and my coat once sleek

Hangs rough and undistinguished on my bones.
O God I was so beautiful when I was well.
My heart, my lungs, my sinews and my reins
Consumed a solitary ecstasy,
And light and pride informed each artery.
Then I a temple, now a charnel house.
Then I a high hozannah, now a dirge.
Then I a recompense of God's endeavour,
Now a reproach and earnest of lost toil.
Consider, Lord, a tiger's melancholy
And heed a minished tiger's muted moan,
For thou art sleek and shining bright
And I am weary.
Thy countenance is full of light
And mine is dreary.

Autumn

He told his life story to Mrs Courtly
Who was a widow. 'Let us get married shortly',
He said. 'I am no longer passionate,
But we can have some conversation before it is too late.'

Bog-Face

Dear little Bog-Face,
Why are you so cold?
And why do you lie with your eyes shut? –
You are not very old.

I am a Child of this World,
And a Child of Grace,
And Mother, I shall be glad when it is over,
I am Bog-Face.

The Zoo

The lion sits within his cage,
Weeping tears of ruby rage,
He licks his snout, the tears fall down
And water dusty London town.

He does not like you, little boy,
It's no use making up to him,
He does not like you any more
Than he likes Nurse, or Baby Jim.

Nor would you do if you were he,
And he were you, for dont you see
God gave him lovely teeth and claws
So that he might eat little boys.

So that he might
In anger slay
The little lambs
That skip and play
Pounce down upon their placid dams
And make dams flesh to pad his hams.

So that he might
Appal the night
With crunching bones
And awful groans
Of antelope and buffalo,
And the unwary hunter whose 'Hallo'
Tells us his life is over here below.
There's none to help him, fear inspired,
Who shouts because his gun misfired.

All this the lion sees, and pants
Because he knows the hot sun slants
Between the rancid jungle-grass,
Which never more shall part to let him pass
Down to the jungle drinking-hole,
Whither the zebra comes with her sleek foal.

The sun is hot by day and has his swink,
And sops up sleepy lions' and tigers' stink,
But not this lion's stink, poor carnivore,
He's on the shady shelf for ever more.

His claws are blunt, his teeth fall out,
No victim's flesh consoles his snout,
And that is why his eyes are red
Considering his talents are misusèd.

Advice to Young Children

'Children who paddle where the ocean bed shelves steeply
Must take great care they do not,
Paddle too deeply.'

Thus spake the awful aging couple
Whose heart the years had turned to rubble.

But the little children, to save any bother,
Let it in at one ear and out at the other.

The Face

There is a face I know too well,
A face I dread to see,
So vain it is, so eloquent
Of all futility.

It is a human face that hides
A monkey soul within,
That bangs about, that beats a gong,
That makes a horrid din.

Sometimes the monkey soul will sprawl
Athwart the human eyes,
And peering forth, will flesh its pads,
And utter social lies.

So wretched is this face, so vain,
So empty and forlorn,
You well may say that better far
This face had not been born.

If I lie down

If I lie down upon my bed I must be here,
But if I lie down in my grave I may be elsewhere.

Conviction (i)

Christ died for God and me
Upon the crucifixion tree
For God a spoken Word
For me a Sword
For God a hymn of praise
For me eternal days
For God an explanation
For me salvation.

Conviction (ii)

I walked abroad in Easter Park,
I heard the wild dog's distant bark,
I knew my Lord was risen again, –
Wild dog, wild dog, you bark in vain.

Conviction (iii)

The shadow was so black,
I thought it was a cat,
But once in to it
I knew it

No more black
Than a shadow's back.

Illusion is a freak
Of mind;
The cat's to seek.

Conviction (iv)

I like to get off with people,
I like to lie in their arms,
I like to be held and tightly kissed,
Safe from all alarms.

I like to laugh and be happy
With a beautiful beautiful kiss,
I tell you, in all the world
There is no bliss like this.

Villains

Profit and Batten
Had coats lined with satin,
And no wonder either,
For they never owed a stiver;
If folks owed them rent,
They owed at ten per cent.
Sing Batten and Profit
If you've got a hat, doff it.

The Little Daughters of America

Pearl Harbor, 1941.

Admirals Curse-You and No-More
Set their compasses and sailed for war.

I am sorry that all the little daughters of America
Should be involved in a thing like this; upon my word.

She said . . .

She said as she tumbled the baby in:
There, little baby, go sink or swim,
I brought you into the world, what more should I do?
Do you expect me always to be responsible for you?

The Conventionalist

Fourteen-year-old, why must you giggle and dote,
Fourteen-year-old, why are you such a goat?
I'm fourteen years old, that is the reason,
I giggle and dote in season.

Study to Deserve Death

Study to deserve Death, they only may
Who fought well upon their earthly day,
Who never sheathed their swords or ran away.

See, such a man as this now proudly stands,
Pale in the clasp of Death, and to his hands
Yields up the sword, but keeps the laurel bands.

Honour and emulate his warrior soul,
For whom the sonorous death-bells toll;
He after journeying has reached his goal.

Prate not to me of suicide,
Faint heart in battle, not for pride
I say Endure, but that such end denied
Makes welcomer yet the death that's to be died.

Dirge

From a friend's friend I taste friendship,
From a friend's friend love,
My spirit in confusion,
Long years I strove,
But now I know that never
Nearer I shall move,
Than a friend's friend to friendship,
To love than a friend's love.

Into the dark night
Resignedly I go,
I am not so afraid of the dark night
As the friends I do not know,
I do not fear the night above,
As I fear the friends below.

Distractions and the Human Crowd

Ormerod was deeply troubled
When he read in philosophy and religion
Of man's lust after God,
And the knowledge of God,
And the experience of God
In the achievement of solitary communion and the loss of self.
For he said that he had known this knowledge,
And experienced this experience,
Before life and after death;
But that here in temporal life, and in temporal life only, was
permitted,
(As in a flaw of divine government, a voluntary recession),

A place where man might impinge upon man,
And be subject to a thousand and one idiotic distractions.
And thus it was that he found himself
Ever at issue with the Schools,
For ever more and more he pursued the distractions,
Knowing them to be ephemeral, under time, peculiar,
And in eternity, without place or puff.
Then, ah then, he said, following the tea-parties,
(And the innumerable conferences for social rearrangement),
I knew, and shall know again, the name of God, closer than
    close;
But now I know a stranger thing,
That never can I study too closely, for never will it come
    again, –
Distractions and the human crowd.

The Wild Dog

The City Dog goes to the drinking trough,
He waves his tail and laughs, and goes when he has had enough.
His intelligence is on the brink
Of human intelligence. He knows the Council will give him a
    drink.

The Wild Dog is not such an animal,
Untouched by human kind, he is inimical,
He keeps his tail stiff, his eyes blink,
And he goes to the river when he wants a drink.
He goes to the river, he stamps on the mud,
And at night he sleeps in the dark wood.

Lady 'Rogue' Singleton

Come, wed me, Lady Singleton,
And we will have a baby soon
And we will live in Edmonton
Where all the friendly people run.

I could never make you happy, darling,
Or give you the baby you want,
I would always very much rather, dear,
Live in a tent.

I am not a cold woman, Henry,
But I do not feel for you,
What I feel for the elephants and the miasmas
And the general view.

Mother

I have a happy nature,
But Mother is always sad,
I enjoy every moment of my life, –
Mother has been had.

The Bottle of Aspirins

'I look at the bottle, when mournful I feel.'
'C'est une ressource contre tout', ajouta-t-il,
(Avec le sombre gaité du pays des suicides
D'où il etait), – 'two hundred and I am freed,'
He said, 'from anxiety.'

The Governess

The milky love of this bland child
Her governess has quite beguiled,
And now they spend the hours talking,
Sometimes winding wool and sometimes walking.

Forgot!

There is a fearful solitude
Within the careless multitude,
And in the open country too,

He mused, and then it seemed to him
The solitude lay all within;
He longed for some interior din:

Some echo from the worldly rout,
To indicate a common lot,
Some charge that he might be about,
But oh he felt that he was quite forgot.

The Broken Heart

'Oh, Sing to me Gypsy.'

He told me he loved me,
He gave me red roses,
Twelve crimson roses
As red as my blood.

The roses he gave me,
The roses are withered,
Twelve crimson roses
As red as my blood.

The roses are withered,
But here on my breast, far
Redder than they is
The red of my heart's blood.

He told me he loved me,
He gave me red roses,
Twelve crimson roses
As red as my blood.

In the Night

I longed for companionship rather,
But my companions I always wished farther.
And now in the desolate night
I think only of the people I should like to bite.

The Poets are Silent

There's no new spirit abroad,
As I looked, I saw;
And I say that it is to the poets' merit
To be silent about the war.

Happiness

Happiness is silent, or speaks equivocally for friends,
Grief is explicit and her song never ends,
Happiness is like England, and will not state a case,
Grief like Guilt rushes in and talks apace.

Lot's Wife

*'In that rich, oil-bearing region, it is probable that Lot's wife was
turned into a pillar of asphalt – not salt.'*

Sir William Whitebait, Member of the Institute of Mining Engineers

I long for the desolate valleys,
Where the rivers of asphalt flow,
For here in the streets of the living,
Where my footsteps run to and fro,
Though my smile be never so friendly,
I offend wherever I go.

Yes, here in the land of the living,
Though a marriage be fairly sprung,
And the heart be loving and giving,
In the end it is sure to go wrong.

Then take me to the valley of asphalt,
And turn me to a river of stone,
That no tree may shift to my sighing,
Or breezes convey my moan.

44

Satin-Clad

Satin–clad, with many a pearl,
Is this rich and wretched girl.
Does she weep? Her tears are crystal,
And she counts them as they fall.

Unpopular, lonely and loving

Unpopular, lonely and loving,
Elinor need not trouble,
For if she were not so loving,
She would not be so miserable.

Voices against England in the Night

'England, you had better go,
There is nothing else that you ought to do,
You lump of survival value, you are too slow.

England, you have been here too long,
And the songs you sing are the songs you sung
On a braver day. Now they are wrong.

And as you sing the sliver slips from your lips,
And the governing garment sits ridiculously on your hips.
It is a pity that you are still too cunning to make slips.'

Dr Goebbels, that is the point,
You are a few years too soon with your jaunt,
Time and the moment is not yet England's daunt.

Yes, dreaming Germany with your Urge and Night,
You must go down before English and American might.
It is well, it is well, cries the peace kite.

Perhaps England our darling will recover her lost thought
We must think sensibly about our victory and not be
    distraught,
Perhaps America will have an idea, and perhaps not.

But they cried: Could not England, once the world's best,
Put off her governing garment and be better dressed
In a shroud, a shroud? O history turn thy pages fast!

'I could let Tom go – but what about the children?'

Since what you want, not what you ought,
Is the difficult thing to decide,
I advise you, Amelia, to persevere
With Duty for your guide.

Torquemada

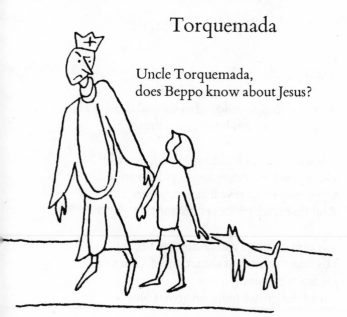

Uncle Torquemada,
does Beppo know about Jesus?

To Dean Inge Lecturing on Origen

Listen, all of you, listen, all of you,
This way wisdom lies,
To reconcile with the simplicity of God
His contingent pluralities.

Oh, the wise man sat in his chair,
And oh, the people they would not hear,
They said, It is much too deep for us,
As they turned to the Differential Calculus.

Oh, if the people had only heard
Him,
Oh, if that wise man's word was not blurred,
Not dimmed.

A Mother's Hearse

The love of a mother for her child
Is not necessarily a beautiful thing
It can be compounded of pride and show
And exalt the self above every thing.

Oh why is that child so spoilt and horrible?
His mother has never neglected the trouble
Of giving him his will at every turn
And that is why his eyes do burn.

His eyes do burn with a hungry fire
His fingers clutch at the air and do not tire
He is a persecuting force
And as he grows older he grows worse.

And for his sake the friends are put down
And the happy people do not come round,
In pride and hostility against the world
This family upon itself is now curled.

Oh wretched they and wretched the friend
And this will continue without end
And all for a mother's love it was,
I say it were better a mother's hearse.

Thought is Superior

Thought is superior to dress and circumstance,
It is thought pure thought that sets the world in a dance.
And what is the greatest thought since the world begun?
Galileo's discovery that the earth goes round the sun.

The River God

I may be smelly, and I may be old,
Rough in my pebbles, reedy in my pools,
But where my fish float by I bless their swimming
And I like the people to bathe in me, especially women.
But I can drown the fools
Who bathe too close to the weir, contrary to rules.
And they take a long time drowning
As I throw them up now and then in a spirit of clowning.
Hi yih, yippity-yap, merrily I flow,

O I may be an old foul river but I have plenty of go.
Once there was a lady who was too bold
She bathed in me by the tall black cliff where the water runs
    cold,
So I brought her down here
To be my beautiful dear.
Oh will she stay with me will she stay
This beautiful lady, or will she go away?
She lies in my beautiful deep river bed with many a weed
To hold her, and many a waving reed.
Oh who would guess what a beautiful white face lies there
Waiting for me to smooth and wash away the fear
She looks at me with. Hi yih, do not let her
Go. There is no one on earth who does not forget her
Now. They say I am a foolish old smelly river
But they do not know of my wide original bed
Where the lady waits, with her golden sleepy head.
If she wishes to go I will not forgive her.

The Orphan Reformed

The orphan is looking for parents
She roams the world over
Looking for parents and cover.
She looks at this pair and that
Cries, Father, Mother,
Likes these, does not like those,
Stays for a time; goes.
Crying, Oh hearts of stone.
But really she is better alone.
Orphan, the people who will not be your
    parents are not evil,

Not the devil.
But still she cries, Father, Mother
Must I be alone for ever?
Yes you must. Oh wicked orphan, oh rebellion,
Must an orphan not be alone is that your opinion?
At last the orphan is reformed. Now quite
Alone she goes; now she is right.
Now when she cries, Father, Mother, it is only to please.
Now the people do not mind, now they
    say she is a mild tease.

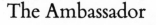

The Ambassador

Underneath the broad hat is the face of the Ambassador
He rides on a white horse through hell looking two ways.
Doors open before him and shut when he has passed.
He is master of the mysteries and in the market place
He is known. He stole the trident, the girdle,
The sword, the sceptre and many mechanical instruments.
Thieves honour him. In the underworld he rides carelessly.
Sometimes he rises into the air and flies silently.

Do Take Muriel Out

Do take Muriel out
She is looking so glum
Do take Muriel out
All her friends have gone.

And after too much pressure
Looking for them in the Palace
She goes home to too much leisure
And this is what her life is.

All her friends are gone
And she is alone
And she looks for them where they have never been
And her peace is flown.

Her friends went into the forest
And across the river
And the desert took their footprints
And they went with a believer.

Ah they are gone they were so beautiful
And she can not come to them
And she kneels in her room at night
Crying, Amen.

Do take Muriel out
Although your name is Death
She will not complain
When you dance her over the blasted heath.

Le Singe Qui Swing

To the tune of Green-sleeves.

Outside the house
The swinging ape
Swung to and fro,
Swung to and fro,
And when midnight shone so clear
He was still swinging there.

Oh ho the swinging ape,
The happy peaceful animal,
Oh ho the swinging ape,
I love to see him gambol.

Pad, pad

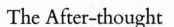

I always remember your beautiful flowers
And the beautiful kimono you wore
When you sat on the couch
With that tigerish crouch
And told me you loved me no more.

What I cannot remember is how I felt when you were unkind
All I know is, if you were unkind now I should not mind.
Ah me, the power to feel exaggerated, angry and sad
The years have taken from me. Softly I go now, pad pad.

The After-thought

Rapunzel Rapunzel let down your hair
It is I your beautiful lover who am here
And when I come up this time I will bring a rope ladder with
    me
And then we can both escape into the dark wood immediately.
This must be one of those things, as Edgar Allan Poe says
    somewhere in a book,
Just because it is perfectly obvious one is certain to overlook.

I wonder sometimes by the way if Poe isn't a bit introspective,
One can stand about getting rather reflective,
But thinking about the way the mind works, you know,
Makes one inactive, one simply doesn't know which way to go;
Like the centipede in the poem who was corrupted by the toad
And ever after never did anything but lie in the middle of the
       road,
Or the old gurus of India I've seen, believe it or not,
Standing seventy five years on their toes until they dropped.
Or Titurel, for that matter, in his odd doom
Crying: I rejoice because by the mercy of the Saviour I
       continue to live in the tomb.

What is that darling? You cannot hear me?
That's odd. I can hear you quite distinctly.

The Wanderer

Twas the voice of the Wanderer, I heard her exclaim,
You have weaned me too soon, you must nurse me again,
She taps as she passes at each window pane,
Pray, does she not know that she taps in vain?

Her voice flies away on the midnight wind,
But would she be happier if she were within?
She is happier far where the night winds fall,
And there are no doors and no windows at all.

No man has seen her, this pitiful ghost,
And no woman either, but heard her at most,
Sighing and tapping and sighing again,
You have weaned me too soon, you must nurse me again.

The Deserter

The world is come upon me, I used to keep it a long way off,
But now I have been run over and I am in the hands of the
    hospital staff.
They say as a matter of fact I have not been run over it's
    imagination,
But they all admit I shall be kept in bed under observation.
I must say it's very comfortable here, nursie has such nice
    hands,
And every morning the doctor come and lances my
    tuberculous glands.
He says he does nothing of the sort, but I have my own feelings
    about that,
And what they are if you don't mind I shall keep under my
    hat.
My friend, if you call it a friend, has left me; he says I am a
    deserter to ill health,
And that the things I should think about have made off for
    ever, and so has my wealth.
Portentous ass, what to do about him's no strain
I shall quite simply never speak to the fellow again.

God and Man

Man is my darling, my love and my pain,
My pleasure, my excitement, and my love again,
My wisdom, my courage, my power, my all,
Oh Man, do not come to me until I call.

In man is my life, and in man is my death,
He is my hazard, my pride and my breath,
I sought him, I wrought him, I pant on his worth,
In him I experience indeterminate growth.

Oh Man, Man, of all my animals dearest,
Do not come till I call, though thou weariest first.

My Cats

I like to toss him up and down
A heavy cat weighs half a Crown
With a hey do diddle my cat Brown.

I like to pinch him on the sly
When nobody is passing by
With a hey do diddle my cat Fry.

I like to ruffle up his pride
And watch him skip and turn aside
With a hey do diddle my cat Hyde.

Hey Brown and Fry and Hyde my cats
That sit on tombstone for your mats.

Drugs Made Pauline Vague

Drugs made Pauline vague.
She sat one day at the breakfast table
Fingering in a baffled way
The fronds of the maidenhair plant.

Was it the salt you were looking for dear?
Said Dulcie, exchanging a glance with the Brigadier.

Chuff chuff Pauline what's the matter?
Said the Brigadier to his wife
Who did not even notice
What a handsome couple they made.

Our Bog is Dood

Our Bog is dood, our Bog is dood,
They lisped in accents mild,
But when I asked them to explain
They grew a little wild.
How do you know your Bog is dood
My darling little child?

We know because we wish it so
That is enough, they cried,
And straight within each infant eye
Stood up the flame of pride,
And if you do not think it so
You shall be crucified.

Then tell me, darling little ones,
What's dood, suppose Bog is?
Just what we think, the answer came,
Just what we think it is.
They bowed their heads. Our Bog is ours
And we are wholly his.

But when they raised them up again
They had forgotten me
Each one upon each other glared
In pride and misery
For what was dood, and what their Bog
They never could agree.

Oh sweet it was to leave them then,
And sweeter not to see,
And sweetest of all to walk alone
Beside the encroaching sea,
The sea that soon should drown them all,
That never yet drowned me.

Wretched Woman

Wretched woman that thou art
How thou piercest to my heart
With thy misery and graft
And thy lack of household craft.

To School!

Let all the little poets be gathered together in classes
And let prizes be given to them by the Prize Asses
And let them be sure to call all the little poets young
And worse follow what's bad begun
But do not expect the Muse to attend this school
Why look already how far off she has flown, she is no fool.

To an American Publisher

You say I must write *another* book? But I've just written this
    one.
You liked it so much that's the reason? Read it again then.

I Am

Far from normal far from normal far from normal I am
He sighed as he stood on the river bank and watched where the
      fishes swam
But ever the wind in the willow trees whispered, I am; I am.
He saw the variety of nature
The ant the mole and the sky
And resignedly hurried upon his way
Crying: I, I; I, I;

Then a priest came and told him if he was good
And thought as he ought and did as he should
He should be saved by the Lamb's fresh blood.

Oh I know, I know the poor man cries,
I know the worth of the heavenly prize
And I know the strength of the race to be run
But my black heart cleaves to the strength of my gun.

Then he put his gun to his head and shot
Crying absurdly, I am not.

Our Office Cat

Our Office cat is a happy cat
She has had two hundred kittens
And every one has been adopted into happy homes
By our cat-loving Britons.

Do Not!

Do not despair of man, and do not scold him,
Who are you that you should so lightly hold him?
Are you not also a man, and in your heart
Are there not warlike thoughts and fear and smart?
Are you not also afraid and in fear cruel,
Do you not think of yourself as usual,
Faint for ambition, desire to be loved,
Prick at a virtuous thought by beauty moved?
You love your wife, you hold your children dear,
Then say not that Man is vile, but say they are.
But they are not. So is your judgement shown
Presumptuous, false, quite vain, merely your own
Sadness for failed ambition set outside,
Made a philosophy of, prinked, beautified
In noble dress and into the world sent out
To run with the ill it most pretends to rout.
Oh know your own heart, that heart's not wholly evil,
And from the particular judge the general,
If judge you must, but with compassion see life,
Or else, of yourself despairing, flee strife.

In Protocreation

In protocreation
Is my imagination
And in the world's first emergence from gaseous fire
My desire.
Then heaved the earth
In a first vegetable birth
Later according to the record
Experimental animals walked abroad.
The awkward pterodactyl
The brontosaurus
The mammoth and the early lizard
Were before us.
Oh had it but stopped then
Oh had there not come men.
Earth fired
And the seas smoked
Heavy heavy swung the swamp
Crust broke and the mountains poked.
Oh had it but stopped then
Oh had there not come men.
In that high and early time
There was no good deed and no crime
No oppression by informed mind
No knowledge and no human kind.

Deeply Morbid

Deeply morbid deeply morbid was the girl who typed the
    letters
Always out of office hours running with her social betters
But when daylight and the darkness of the office closed
    about her
Not for this ah not for this her office colleagues came to doubt
    her
It was that look within her eye
Why did it always seem to say goodbye?

Joan her name was and at lunchtime
Solitary solitary
She would go and watch the pictures
In the National Gallery
All alone all alone
This time with no friend beside her
She would go and watch the pictures
All alone.

Will she leave her office colleagues
Will she leave her evening pleasures
Toil within a friendly bureau
Running later in her leisure?
All alone all alone
Before the pictures she seems turned to stone.

Close upon the Turner pictures
Closer than a thought may go
Hangs her eye and all the colours
Leap into a special glow
All for her, all alone
All for her, all for Joan.

First the canvas where the ocean
Like a mighty animal
With a really wicked motion
Leaps for sailors' funeral

Holds her panting. Oh the creature
Oh the wicked virile thing
With its skin of fleck and shadow
Stretching tightening over him.
Wild yet captured wild yet captured
By the painter, Joan is quite enraptured.

Now she edges from the canvas
To another loved more dearly
Where the awful light of purest
Sunshine falls across the spray,
There the burning coasts of fancy
Open to her pleasure lay.
All alone, all alone
Come away, come away
All alone.

Lady Mary, Lady Kitty
The Honourable Featherstonehaugh
Polly Tommy from the office
Which of these shall hold her now?
Come away, come away
All alone.

The spray reached out and sucked her in
It was a hardly noticed thing
That Joan was there and is not now

(Oh go and tell young Featherstonehaugh)
Gone away, gone away
All alone.

She stood up straight
The sun fell down
There was no more of London Town
She went upon the painted shore
And there she walks for ever more
Happy quite
Beaming bright
In a happy happy light
All alone.

They say she was a morbid girl, no doubt of it
And what befell her clearly grew out of it
But I say she's a lucky one
To walk for ever in that sun
And as I bless sweet Turner's name
I wish that I could do the same.

Not Waving but Drowning

Nobody heard him, the dead man,
But still he lay moaning:
I was much further out than you thought
And not waving but drowning.

Poor chap, he always loved larking
And now he's dead
It must have been too cold for him his heart gave way,
They said.

Oh, no no no, it was too cold always
(Still the dead one lay moaning)
I was much too far out all my life
And not waving but drowning.

The New Age

Shall I tell you the signs of a New Age coming?
It is a sound of drubbing and sobbing
Of people crying, We are old, we are old
And the sun is going down and becoming cold
Oh sinful and sad and the last of our kind
If we turn to God now do you think He will mind?
Then they fall on their knees and begin to whine
That the state of Art itself presages decline
As if Art has anything or ever had
To do with civilization whether good or bad.
Art is wild as a cat and quite separate from civilization
But that is another matter that is not now under consideration.
Oh these people are fools with their sighing and sinning
Why should Man be at an end? he is hardly beginning.
This New Age will slip in under cover of their cries
And be upon them before they have opened their eyes.
Well, say geological time is a one-foot rule
Then Man's only been here about half an inch to play the fool
Or be wise if he likes, as he often has been
Oh heavens how these crying people spoil the beautiful
  geological scene.

A Dream of Comparison

After reading Book Ten of 'Paradise Lost'.

Two ladies walked on the soft green grass
On the bank of a river by the sea
And one was Mary and the other Eve
And they talked philosophically.

'Oh to be Nothing,' said Eve, 'oh for a
Cessation of consciousness
With no more impressions beating in
Of various experiences.'

'How can Something envisage Nothing?' said Mary,
'Where's your philosophy gone?'
'Storm back through the gates of Birth,' cried Eve,
'Where were you before you were born?'

Mary laughed: 'I love Life,
I would fight to the death for it,
That's a feeling you say? I will find
A reason for it.'

They walked by the estuary,
Eve and the Virgin Mary,
And they talked until nightfall,
But the difference between them was radical.

My Hat

Mother said if I wore this hat
I should be certain to get off with the right sort of chap
Well look where I am now, on a desert island
With so far as I can see no one at all on hand
I know what has happened though I suppose Mother
    wouldn't see
This hat being so strong has completely run away with me
I had the feeling it was beginning to happen the moment I put
    it on
What a moment that was as I rose up, I rose up like a flying
    swan
As strong as a swan too, why see how far my hat has flown me
    away
It took us a night to come and then a night and a day
And all the time the swan wing in my hat waved beautifully
Ah, I thought, How this hat becomes me.
First the sea was dark but then it was pale blue
And still the wing beat and we flew and we flew
A night and a day and a night, and by the old right way
Between the sun and the moon we flew until morning day.
It is always early morning here on this peculiar island
The green grass grows into the sea on the dipping land
Am I glad I am here? Yes, well, I am,
It's nice to be rid of Father, Mother and the young man
There's just one thing causes me a twinge of pain,
If I take my hat off, shall I find myself home again?
So in this early morning land I always wear my hat
Go home, you see, well I wouldn't run a risk like that.

70

The Engine Drain

A Fenland Memory.

It was the mighty Engine Drain, the Engine Drain, the Engine
    Drain,
Down which the water went, the water went, the mighty
    waters of the inland sea.
But still in memory I see, the inland sea, the inland sea
That did reflect the summer sky, when it was summer time,
    of Cambridgeshire.
The sky was blue, the sea was blue, the inland sea, the inland
    sea,
All blue and flat and blue and flat it lay for all to see.
The trees stood up, the reeds stood too, and were reflected in
    the mere
As you might call that inland sea, you might have said it was
    a mere.
And in and out the branches all
The little birds did swoop and swing
Did swoop and swing and call
And oh it was a pretty thing to see them swoop and swing.
Oh ho the inland sea, the inland sea, the mighty mere that
    moved so prettily.

When winter came the water rose,
And rose and rose and rose and rose
And all about the cottage floors
It flowed and rose and flowed and rose
Till in their beds at night you'd see
Quite half afloat the midnight peasantry
That got their living hardily
And died of ripe old age rheumatically,
Oh it was quite surprising how
They'd live to ripe old age rheumatically.
It was because they early learnt
To put their boots on properly
While still in bed, while still in bed.

They learnt to put their boots on properly
Afloat in bed upon the inland sea.

And now I do remember how
Looking from shallow banks below
You'd see the little water-snakes
A-swimming to and fro,
So many little water-snakes
Careering round about
No man might stand to count them there
Careering in the pretty mere.

Oh it was merry in that day
To see the water-fowl play
Upon the inland sea,
Chip-chopping in the sea;
Or see them ride the water-race
In winter, till the winds in chase
Drove them ashore. Oh ho the wind upon the mere
It wound the waves in heaps and tossed the spray
That was half froze, upon the darkening day
Whipping the waters up till you might see
A mile away the whitecaps of the inland sea,
The whitecaps of the mere.

Ah me alas the day is past, is past and long ago
And no man living now may say he saw the waters flow,
All all are gone, the Engine Drain
Has took them to the cruel salt sea
And what is left behind?
A fertile flat and farming land,
A profitable farming land
Is what is left behind.
It took some time, as you might guess,
But not so long as you would guess,
A day or two, or two or three,
To take these waters to the sea
To take them to the Wash.

Why was it called the Engine Drain, the Engine Drain, the
     Engine Drain?
It was because the others were,
The other drains of Cambridgeshire,
Controlled by air, by windmills blowing there.
But oh this Engine was a force, a mighty engineering force,
It took the waters of the mere and brought them to the Wash,
It took them, did the Engine Drain, these waters of the inland
     sea,
And droppt 'em in the cruel salt sea,
The cruel salt sea.

Songe d'Athalie

From Racine.

It was a dream and shouldn't I bother about a dream?
But it goes on you know, tears me rather.
Of course I try to forget it but it will not let me.
Well it was on an extraordinarily dark night at midnight
My mother Queen Jezebel appeared suddenly before me
Looking just as she did the day she died, dressed grandly.
It was her pride you noticed, nothing she had gone through
     touched that
And she still had the look of being most carefully made up
She always made up a lot she didn't want people to know how
     old she was.
She spoke: Be warned my daughter, true girl to me, she said,
Do not suppose the cruel God of the Jews has finished with
     you,
I am come to weep your falling into his hands, my child.
With these appalling words my mother,
This ghost, leant over me stretching out her hands
And I stretched out my hands too to touch her
But what was it, oh this is horrible, what did I touch?
Nothing but the mangled flesh and the breaking bones
Of a body that the dogs tearing quarrelled over.

73

Away, Melancholy

Away, melancholy,
Away with it, let it go.

Are not the trees green,
The earth as green?
Does not the wind blow,
Fire leap and the rivers flow?
Away melancholy.

The ant is busy
He carrieth his meat,
All things hurry
To be eaten or eat.
Away, melancholy.

Man, too, hurries,
Eats, couples, buries,
He is an animal also
With a hey ho melancholy,
Away with it, let it go.

Man of all creatures
Is superlative
(Away melancholy)
He of all creatures alone
Raiseth a stone
(Away melancholy)
Into the stone, the god
Pours what he knows of good
Calling, good, God.
Away melancholy, let it go.

Speak not to me of tears,
Tyranny, pox, wars,
Saying, Can God
Stone of man's thought, be good?

Say rather it is enough
That the stuffed
Stone of man's good, growing,
By man's called God.
Away, melancholy, let it go.

Man aspires
To good,
To love
Sighs;

Beaten, corrupted, dying
In his own blood lying
Yet heaves up an eye above
Cries, Love, love.
It is his virtue needs explaining,
Not his failing.

Away, melancholy,
Away with it, let it go.

Childle Rolandine

Dark was the day for Childe Rolandine the artist
When she went to work as a secretary-typist
And as she worked she sang this song
Against oppression and the rule of wrong:

It is the privilege of the rich
To waste the time of the poor
To water with tears in secret
A tree that grows in secret
That bears fruit in secret
That ripened falls to the ground in secret
And manures the parent tree
Oh the wicked tree of hatred and the secret
The sap rising and the tears falling.

Likely also, sang the Childe, my soul will fry in hell
Because of this hatred, while in heaven my employer does well
And why should he not, exacerbating though he be but generous
Is it his fault I must work at a work that is tedious?
Oh heaven sweet heaven keep my thoughts in their night den
Do not let them by day be spoken.

But then she sang, Ah why not? tell all, speak, speak,
Silence is vanity, speak for the whole truth's sake.

And rising she took the bugle and put it to her lips, crying:
There is a Spirit feeds on our tears, I give him mine,
Mighty human feelings are his food
Passion and grief and joy his flesh and blood
That he may live and grow fat we daily die
This cropping One is our immortality.

Childe Rolandine bowed her head and in the evening
Drew the picture of the spirit from heaven.

The Jungle Husband

Dearest Evelyn, I often think of you
Out with the guns in the jungle stew
Yesterday I hittapotamus
I put the measurements down for you but they got lost in the
    fuss
It's not a good thing to drink out here
You know, I've practically given it up dear.
Tomorrow I am going alone a long way
Into the jungle. It is all gray
But green on top
Only sometimes when a tree has fallen
The sun comes down plop, it is quite appalling.
You never want to go in a jungle pool
In the hot sun, it would be the act of a fool
Because it's always full of anacondas, Evelyn, not looking
    ill-fed
I'll say. So no more now, from your loving husband, Wilfred.

Why are the Clergy . . . ?

Why are the clergy of the Church of England
Always altering the words of the prayers in the Prayer Book?
Cranmer's touch was surer than theirs, do they not respect
    him?
For instance last night in church I heard
(I italicize the interpolation)
'The Lord bless you and keep you *and all who are dear unto you*'
As the blessing is a congregational blessing and meant to be
This is questionable on theological grounds
But is it not offensive to the ear and also ludicrous?
That 'unto' is a particularly ripe piece of idiocy
Oh how offensive it is. I suppose we shall have next
'Lighten our darkness we beseech thee oh Lord *and the darkness
    of all who are dear unto us.*'
It seems a pity. Does Charity object to the objection?
Then I cry, and not for the first time to that smooth face
Charity, have pity.

But Murderous

A mother slew her unborn babe
In a day of recent date
Because she did not wish him to be born in a world
Of murder and war and hate
'Oh why should I bear a babe from my womb
To be broke in pieces by the hydrogen bomb?'

I say this woman deserves little pity
That she was a fool and a murderess
Is a child's destiny to be contained by a mind
That signals only a lady in distress?

And why should human infancy be so superior
As to be too good to be born in this world?
Did she think it was an angel or a baa-lamb
That lay in her belly furled?

Oh the child is the young of its species
Alike with that noble, vile, curious and fierce
How foolish this poor mother to suppose
Her act told us aught that was not murderous

(As, item, That the arrogance of a half-baked mind
Breeds murder; makes us all unkind.)

This is Disgraceful and Abominable

Of all the disgraceful and abominable things
Making animals perform for the amusement of human beings is
Utterly disgraceful and abominable.

Animals are animals and have their nature
And that's enough, it is enough, leave it alone.

A disgraceful and abominable thing I saw in a French circus
A performing dog

Raised his back leg when he did not need to
He did not wish to relieve himself, he was made to raise his leg.
The people sniggered. Oh how disgraceful and abominable.
Weep for the disgrace, forbid the abomination.
The animals are cruelly trained,
How could patience do it, it would take too long, they are
      cruelly trained.
Lions leap through fire, it is offensive,
Elephants dance, it is offensive
That the dignified elephant should dance for fear of hot plates,
The lion leap or be punished.
And how can the animals be quartered or carted except
      cheaply?
Profit lays on the whip of punishment, money heats the
      prodding iron,
Cramps cages. Oh away with it, away with it, it is so disgraceful
      and abominable.
Weep the disgraces. Forbid the abominations.

God the Eater

There is a god in whom I do not believe
Yet to this god my love stretches,
This god whom I do not believe in is
My whole life, my life and I am his.

Everything that I have of pleasure and pain
(Of pain, of bitter pain and men's contempt)
I give this god for him to feed upon
As he is my whole life and I am his.

When I am dead I hope that he will eat
Everything I have been and have not been
And crunch and feed upon it and grow fat
Eating my life all up as it is his.

The Airy Christ

After reading Dr Rieu's translation of St Mark's Gospel.

Who is this that comes in splendour, coming from the blazing
    East?
This is he we had not thought of, this is he the airy Christ.

Airy, in an airy manner in an airy parkland walking,
Others take him by the hand, lead him, do the talking.

But the Form, the airy One, frowns an airy frown,
What they say he knows must be, but he looks aloofly down,

Looks aloofly at his feet, looks aloofly at his hands,
Knows they must, as prophets say, nailèd be to wooden bands.

As he knows the words he sings, that he sings so happily
Must be changed to working laws, yet sings he ceaselessly.

Those who truly hear the voice, the words, the happy song,
Never shall need working laws to keep from doing wrong.

Deaf men will pretend sometimes they hear the song, the words,
And make excuse to sin extremely; this will be absurd.

Heed it not. Whatever foolish men may do the song is cried
For those who hear, and the sweet singer does not care that he
    was crucified.

For he does not wish that men should love him more than
    anything
Because he died; he only wishes they would hear him sing.

The Celts

I think of the Celts as rather a whining lady
Who was beautiful once but is not so much so now
She is not very loving, but there is one thing she loves
It is her grievance which she hugs and takes out walking.

The Celtic lady likes fighting very much for freedom
But when she has got it she is a proper tyrant
Nobody likes her much when she is governing.

The Celtic lady is not very widely popular
But the English love her oh they love her very much
Especially when the Celtic lady is Irish they love her
Which is odd as she hates them then more than anyone else.
When she's Welsh the English stupidly associate her chiefly
With national hats, eisteddfods and Old Age Pensions.
(They don't think of her at all when she is Scotch, it is rather
    a problem.)

Oh the Celtic lady when she's Irish is the one for me
Oh she is so witty and wild, my word witty,
And flashing and spiteful this Celtic lady we love
All the same she is not so beautiful as she was.

Cat Asks Mouse Out

Mrs Mouse
Come out of your house
It is a fine sunny day
And I am waiting to play.

Bring the little mice too
And we can run to and fro.

Loin de l'Être

You don't look at all well, quite loin de l'être in fact
Poor pale-face what's the matter, don't they know?
Oh they don't know, but still I don't feel well
Nor ever shall, my name is *Loin de l'Être*.

They stood on the empty terrace above the precipice
When this conversation took place
Between the affectionate but exasperated friend
And the invalid. It is not possible to be
Ill and merry, poor *Loin de l'Être* sighed
And forced a smile, but oh she was so tired.
So tired, called Echo, so tired.

Now pull yourself together, cried the friend
Together cried Echo,
I must leave you now for a tick, she said
Mind you don't get edgy looking at the precipice.
The lovely invalid sighed, Loin de l'être,
And Echo taking the form of a handsome young man
Cried, *Loin de l'Être* and took her away with him.

My Cat Major

Major is a fine cat
What is he at?
He hunts birds in the hydrangea
And in the tree
Major was ever a ranger
He ranges where no one can see.

Sometimes he goes up to the attic
With a hooped back
His paws hit the iron rungs
Of the ladder in a quick kick
How can this be done?
It is a knack.

Oh Major is a fine cat
He walks cleverly
And what is he at, my fine cat?
No one can see.

The English

Many of the English,
The intelligent English,
Of the Arts, the Professions and the Upper Middle Classes,
Are under-cover men,
But what is under the cover
(That was original)
Died; now they are corpse-carriers.
It is not noticeable, but be careful,
They are infective.

The Past

People who are always praising the past
And especially the times of faith as best
Ought to go and live in the Middle Ages
And be burnt at the stake as witches and sages.

Longing for Death because of Feebleness

Oh would that I were a reliable spirit careering around
Congenially employed and no longer by *feebleness* bound
Oh who would not leave the flesh to become a reliable spirit
Possibly travelling far and acquiring merit.

Magna est Veritas

With my looks I am bound to look simple or fast I would
      rather look simple
So I wear a tall hat on the back of my head that is rather a temple
And I walk rather queerly and comb my long hair
And people say, Don't bother about her.
So in my time I have picked up a good many facts,
Rather more than the people do who wear smart hats
And I do not deceive because I am rather simple too
And although I collect facts I do not always know what they
      amount to.
I regard them as a contribution to almighty Truth, magna est
      veritas et praevalebit,
Agreeing with that Latin writer, Great is Truth and will
      prevail in a bit.

Jumbo

Jumbo, Jumbo, Jumbo darling, Jumbo come to Mother.
But Jumbo wouldn't, he was a dog who simply wouldn't
      bother
An ugly beast he was with drooping guts and filthy skin,
It was quite wonderful how 'mother' loved the ugly thing.

Thoughts about the Person from Porlock

Coleridge received the Person from Porlock
And ever after called him a curse,
Then why did he hurry to let him in?
He could have hid in the house.

It was not right of Coleridge in fact it was wrong
(But often we all do wrong)
As the truth is I think he was already stuck
With Kubla Khan.

He was weeping and wailing: I am finished, finished,
I shall never write another word of it,
When along comes the Person from Porlock
And takes the blame for it.

It was not right, it was wrong,
But often we all do wrong.

*

May we inquire the name of the Person from Porlock?
Why, Porson, didn't you know?
He lived at the bottom of Porlock Hill
So had a long way to go,

He wasn't much in the social sense
Though his grandmother was a Warlock,
One of the Rutlandshire ones I fancy
And nothing to do with Porlock,

And he lived at the bottom of the hill as I said
And had a cat named Flo,
And had a cat named Flo.

I long for the Person from Porlock
To bring my thoughts to an end,
I am becoming impatient to see him
I think of him as a friend,

Often I look out of the window
Often I run to the gate
I think, He will come this evening,
I think it is rather late.

I am hungry to be interrupted
For ever and ever amen
O Person from Porlock come quickly
And bring my thoughts to an end.

*

I felicitate the people who have a Person from Porlock
To break up everything and throw it away
Because then there will be nothing to keep them
And they need not stay.

*

Why do they grumble so much?
He comes like a benison
They should be glad he has not forgotten them
They might have had to go on.

*

These thoughts are depressing I know. They are depressing,
I wish I was more cheerful, it is more pleasant,
Also it is a duty, we should smile as well as submitting
To the purpose of One Above who is experimenting
With various mixtures of human character which goes best,
All is interesting for him it is exciting, but not for us.
There I go again. Smile, smile, and get some work to do
Then you will be practically unconscious without positively
    having to go.

Recognition not Enough

Sin recognized – but that – may keep us humble,
But oh, it keeps us nasty.

Was He Married ?

Was he married, did he try
To support as he grew less fond of them
Wife and family?

No,
He never suffered such a blow.

Did he feel pointless, feeble and distrait,
Unwanted by everyone and in the way?

From his cradle he was purposeful,
His bent strong and his mind full.

Did he love people very much
Yet find them die one day?

He did not love in the human way.

Did he ask how long it would go on,
Wonder if Death could be counted on for an end?

He did not feel like this,
He had a future of bliss.

Did he never feel strong
Pain for being wrong?

He was not wrong, he was right,
He suffered from others', not his own, spite.

But there *is* no suffering like having made a mistake
Because of being of an inferior make.

He was not inferior,
He was superior.

He knew then that power corrupts but some must govern?

His thoughts were different.

Did he lack friends? Worse,
Think it was for his fault, not theirs?

He did not lack friends,
He had disciples he moulded to his ends.

Did he feel over-handicapped sometimes, yet must draw even?

How could he feel like this? He was the King of Heaven.

. . . find a sudden brightness one day in everything
Because a mood had been conquered, or a sin?

I tell you, he did not sin.

Do only human beings suffer from the irritation
I have mentioned? learn too that being comical
Does not ameliorate the desperation?

Only human beings feel this,
It is because they are so mixed.

All human beings should have a medal,
A god cannot carry it, he is not able.

A god is Man's doll, you ass,
He makes him up like this on purpose.

He might have made him up worse.

He often has, in the past.

To choose a god of love, as he did and does,
Is a little move then?

Yes, it is.

A larger one will be when men
Love love and hate hate but do not deify them?

It will be a larger one.

Poor Soul, poor Girl !

A Débutante.

I cannot imagine anything nicer
Than to be struck by lightning and killed suddenly crossing a
      field
As if somebody cared.
Nobody cares whether I am alive or dead.

Admire Cranmer !

Admire the old man, admire him, admire him,
Mocked by the priests of Mary Tudor, given to the flames,
Flinching and overcoming the flinching, Cranmer.

Admire the martyrs of Bloody Mary's reign,
In the shocking arithmetic of cruel average, ninety
A year, three-hundred; admire them.

But still I cry: Admire the Archbishop,
The old man, the scholar, admire him.
Not simply, for flinching and overcoming simply,
But for his genius, admire him,
His delicate feelings of genius, admire him,

That wrote the Prayer Book
(Admire him !)
And made the flames burn crueller. Admire Cranmer !

God Speaks

I made Man with too many faults. Yet I love him.
And if he wishes, I have a home above for him.
I should like him to be happy. I am genial.
He should not paint me as if I were abominable.
As for instance, that I had a son and gave him for their
　　salvation.
This is one of the faults I meant. It leads to nervous
　　prostration.
All the same, there is a difficulty. I should like him to be
　　happy in heaven here,
But he cannot come by wishing. Only by being already at
　　home here.

Edmonton, thy cemetery . . .

Edmonton, thy cemetery
In which I love to tread
Has roused in me a dreary thought
For all the countless dead,
Ah me, the countless dead.

Yet I believe that one is one
And shall for ever be,
And while I hold to this belief
I walk, oh cemetery,
Thy footpaths happily.

And I believe that two and two
Are but an earthly sum
Whose totalling has no part at all
In heavenly kingdom-come,
I love the dead, I cry, I love
Each happy happy one.

Till Doubt returns with dreary face
And fills my heart with dread
For all the tens and tens and tens
That must make up a hundred,
And I begin to sing with him
As if Belief had never been
Ah me, the countless dead, ah me
The countless countless dead.

My Muse

My Muse sits forlorn
She wishes she had not been born
She sits in the cold
No word she says is ever told.

Why does my Muse only speak when she is unhappy?
She does not, I only listen when I am unhappy
When I am happy I live and despise writing
For my Muse this cannot but be dispiriting.

The Frog Prince

I am a frog
I live under a spell
I live at the bottom
Of a green well

And here I must wait
Until a maiden places me
On her royal pillow
And kisses me
In her father's palace.

The story is familiar
Everybody knows it well
But do other enchanted people feel as nervous
As I do? The stories do not tell,

Ask if they will be happier
When the changes come
As already they are fairly happy
In a frog's doom?

I have been a frog now
For a hundred years
And in all this time
I have not shed many tears,

I am happy, I like the life,
Can swim for many a mile
(When I have hopped to the river)
And am for ever agile.

And the quietness,
Yes, I like to be quiet
I am habituated
To a quiet life,

But always when I think these thoughts
As I sit in my well
Another thought comes to me and says:
It is part of the spell

To be happy
To work up contentment
To make much of being a frog
To fear disenchantment

Says, It will be *heavenly*
To be set free,
Cries, *Heavenly* the girl who disenchants
And the royal times, *heavenly*,
And I think it will be.

Come then, royal girl and royal times,
Come quickly,

I can be happy until you come
But I cannot be heavenly,
Only disenchanted people
Can be heavenly.

Tenuous and Precarious

Tenuous and Precarious
Were my guardians,
Precarious and Tenuous,
Two Romans.

My father was Hazardous,
Hazardous,
Dear old man,
Three Romans.

There was my brother Spurious,
Spurious Posthumous,
Spurious was spurious
Was four Romans.

My husband was Perfidious,
He was perfidious,
Five Romans.

Surreptitious, our son,
Was surreptitious,
He was six Romans.

Our cat Tedious
Still lives,
Count not Tedious
Yet.

My name is Finis,
Finis, Finis,
I am Finis,
Six, five, four, three, two,
One Roman,
Finis.

A House of Mercy

It was a house of female habitation,
Two ladies fair inhabited the house,
And they were brave. For although Fear knocked loud
Upon the door, and said he must come in,
They did not let him in.

There were also two feeble babes, two girls,
That Mrs S. had by her husband had,
He soon left them and went away to sea,
Nor sent them money, nor came home again
Except to borrow back
Her Naval Officer's Wife's Allowance from Mrs S.
Who gave it him at once, she thought she should.

There was also the ladies' aunt
And babes' great aunt, a Mrs Martha Hearn Clode,
And she was elderly.
These ladies put their money all together
And so we lived.

I was the younger of the feeble babes
And when I was a child my mother died
And later Great Aunt Martha Hearn Clode died
And later still my sister went away.

Now I am old I tend my mother's sister
The noble aunt who so long tended us,
Faithful and True her name is. Tranquil.
Also Sardonic. And I tend the house.

It is a house of female habitation
A house expecting strength as it is strong
A house of aristocratic mould that looks apart
When tears fall; counts despair
Derisory. Yet it has kept us well. For all its faults,
If they are faults, of sternness and reserve,
It is a Being of warmth I think; at heart
A house of mercy.

Exeat

I remember the Roman Emperor, one of the cruellest of them,
Who used to visit for pleasure his poor prisoners cramped in
    dungeons,
So then they would beg him for death, and then he would say:
Oh no, oh no, we are not yet friends enough.
He meant they were not yet friends enough for him to give
    them death.
So I fancy my Muse says, when I wish to die:
Oh no, Oh no, we are not yet friends enough,

And Virtue also says:
We are not yet friends enough.

How can a poet commit suicide
When he is still not listening properly to his Muse,
Or a lover of Virtue when
He is always putting her off until tomorrow?

Yet a time may come when a poet or any person
Having a long life behind him, pleasure and sorrow,
But feeble now and expensive to his country
And on the point of no longer being able to make a decision
May fancy Life comes to him with love and says:
We are friends enough now for me to give you death;
Then he may commit suicide, then
He may go.

The True Tyrant
or
The Spirit of Duty Rebuked

Oh my darling Goosey-Gander
Why do you always wish to wander
Evermore, evermore?

Now I have you safe at home
I will never let you roam
Ever more.

Then cried the lady from her kitchen
Standing in her chains of grass:
It is not Duty, it is Love
That will not let me pass
Evermore, evermore
Through the grass-enchainèd door,
    the grassy door.

Oh Christianity, Christianity

Oh Christianity, Christianity,
Why do you not answer our difficulties?
If He was God He was not like us,
He could not lose.

Can Perfection be less than perfection?
Can the creator of the Devil be bested by him?
What can the temptation to possess the earth have meant to
    Him
Who made and possessed it? What do you mean?

And Sin, how could He take our sins upon Him? What does
    it mean?
To take sin upon one is not the same
As to have sin inside one and feel guilty.

It is horrible to feel guilty,
We feel guilty because we are.
Was He horrible? Did He feel guilty?

You say He was born humble – but He was not,
He was born God –
Taking our nature upon Him. But then you say,
He was Perfect Man. Do you mean
Perfectly Man, meaning wholly; or Man without sin? Ah
Perfect Man without sin is not what we are.

Do you mean He did not know that He was God,
Did not know He was the Second Person of the Trinity?
(Oh, if He knew this, and was,
It was a source of strength for Him we do not have)
But this theology of 'emptying' you preach sometimes –
That He emptied Himself of knowing He was God – seems
A theology of false appearances
To mock your facts, as He was God, whether He knew He was
    or not.

Oh what do you mean, what do you mean?
You never answer our difficulties.

You say, Christianity, you say
That the Trinity is unchanging from eternity,
But then you say
At the incarnation He took
Our Manhood into the Godhead,
That did not have it before,
So it must have altered it,
Having it.

Oh what do you mean, what do you mean?
You never answer our questions.

I had a dream . . .

I had a dream I was Helen of Troy
In looks, age and circumstance,
But otherwise I was myself.

It was the ninth year of the siege
And I did not love anybody very much
Except perhaps Cassandra,

103

It was those peculiar eyes she had
As if she were short-sighted
That made me feel I could talk to her,
I would have loved anybody I could talk to.
I suppose you know how it's going to end, I said,
As well as I do? Dreams, dreams? They aren't dreams
You know. Do you know?

I used to walk on the walls
And look towards the Grecian tents . . .
It's odd, I said (to Cassandra, of course) how
Everything one has ever read about Troy
As they have always been such splendid writers who were
        writing
Naturally gets into one's conversation . . .
Where Cressid lay that night, except they did not say
How beastly Scamander looks under this sort of sky,
And the black Greek ships piled up on the seashore beyond
Like prison hulks, like slugs. So there we were
On the walls of Troy. But what I did not know,
And I could not get Cassandra to say either,
Was which of the Helen legends I was,
The phantom, with the real Helen in Egypt,
Or the flesh-and-blood one here
That Menelaus would take back to Sparta.
Remembering this, that there was still some uncertainty,
Raised my spirits. I must say
Dispiritedness was what we were all sunk in,
And though the Royal Family may have seemed spectral
Their dispiritedness was substantial enough, and I dare say
The Greeks were in much the same case, dispirited;
Well, nine years there had been of it, and now
The heavy weather, and the smells
From the battlefield, when the wind was in that direction,
And the spirit of the men, too, on both sides,
This was substantial enough; it seemed to me
Like the spirit of all armies, on all plains, in all wars, the men
No longer thinking why they were there

Or caring, but going on; like the song the English used to sing
In the first world war: We're here because, we're here because,
We're here because, we're here. This was the only time
I heard Cassandra laugh, when I sung this to her. I said:
There you are, you laugh; that shows you are not nearly so
Religious as you think. That's blasphemous, that laugh,
Sets you free. But then she got frightened. All right, I said,
Don't be free, go along and finish up on Clytemnestra's
    sword-point,
Pinked like a good girl. I used to get so cross.
Paris was stupid, it was impossible to talk to him.
Hector might have been different, at least he understood
    enough
To be offended – fear of the gods again, I suppose – because
When I said: Well, you know what the Trojan Women
Are going to say about the sack of Troy and being led away
Into captivity, they are going to say: If these things
Had not happened to us we should not be remembered. I
    hope that
Will be a comfort to you. He was angry and said
I should bring ill luck to Troy by my impiety, so I laughed
But I felt more like crying. I went into our palace then
And into my own room. But the heaviness of the sky
Still oppressed me, and the sad colours of rust and blood
I saw everywhere, as Cassandra saw too. Oh, I thought,
It is an ominous eternal moment I am captive in, it is always
This heavy weather, these colours, and the smell of the dead
    men.
It is curious to be caught in a moment of pause like this,
As a river pauses before it plunges in a great waterfall.
I was at home with these people at least in this, that we
    wished
It was over and done with. But oh, Cassandra, I said,
    catching hold of her,
For she was running away, I shall never make
That mischievous laughing Helen, who goes home with
    Menelaus

And over her needlework, in the quiet palace, laughs,
Telling her story, and cries: Oh shameful me. I am only at
    home
In this moment of pause, where feelings, colours and spirits
    are substantial,
But people are ghosts. When the pause finishes
I shall wake.

Emily writes such a good letter

Mabel was married last week
So now only Tom left

The doctor didn't like Arthur's cough
I have been in bed since Easter

A touch of the old trouble

I am downstairs today
As I write this
I can hear Arthur roaming overhead

He loves to roam
Thank heavens he has plenty of space to roam in

We have seven bedrooms
And an annexe

Which leaves a flat for the chauffeur and his wife

We have much to be thankful for

The new vicar came yesterday
People say he brings a breath of fresh air

He leaves me cold
I do not think he is a gentleman

Yes, I remember Maurice very well
Fancy getting married at his age
She must be a fool

You knew May had moved?
Since Edward died she has been much alone

It was cancer

No, I know nothing of Maud
I never wish to hear her name again
In my opinion Maud
Is an evil woman

Our char has left
And a good riddance too
Wages are very high in Tonbridge

Write and tell me how you are, dear,
And the girls,
Phoebe and Rose
They must be a great comfort to you
Phoebe and Rose.

To Carry the Child

To carry the child into adult life
Is good? I say it is not,
To carry the child into adult life
Is to be handicapped.

The child in adult life is defenceless
And if he is grown-up, knows it,
And the grown-up looks at the childish part
And despises it.

The child, too, despises the clever grown-up,
The man-of-the-world, the frozen,
For the child has the tears alive on his cheek
And the man has none of them.

As the child has colours, and the man sees no
Colours or anything,
Being easy only in things of the mind,
The child is easy in feeling.

Easy in feeling, easily excessive
And in excess powerful,
For instance, if you do not speak to the child
He will make trouble.

You would say a man had the upper hand
Of the child, if a child survive,
I say the child has fingers of strength
To strangle the man alive.

Oh it is not happy, it is never happy,
To carry the child into adulthood,
Let children lie down before full growth
And die in their infanthood

And be guilty of no man's blood.

But oh the poor child, the poor child, what can he do,
Trapped in a grown-up carapace,
But peer outside of his prison room
With the eye of an anarchist?

Company

Rise from your bed of languor
Rise from your bed of dismay
Your friends will not come tomorrow
As they did not come today

You must rely on yourself, they said,
You must rely on yourself,
Oh but I find this pill so bitter said the poor man
As he took it from the shelf

Crying, Oh sweet Death come to me
Come to me for company,
Sweet Death it is only you I can
Constrain for company.

Valuable

After reading two paragraphs in a newspaper.

All these illegitimate babies . . .
Oh girls, girls,
Silly little cheap things,
Why do you not put some value on yourselves,
Learn to say, No?
Did nobody teach you?
Nobody teaches anybody to say No nowadays,
People should teach people to say No.

Oh poor panther,
Oh you poor black animal,
At large for a few moments in a school for young children in
      Paris,
Now in your cage again,
How your great eyes bulge with bewilderment,
There is something there that accuses us,
In your angry and innocent eyes,
Something that says:
I am too valuable to be kept in a cage.

Oh these illegitimate babies!
Oh girls, girls,
Silly little valuable things,
You should have said, No, I am valuable,
And again, It is because I am valuable
I say, No.

Nobody teaches anybody they are valuable nowadays.

Girls, you are valuable,
And you, Panther, you are valuable,
But the girls say: I shall be alone

If I say 'I am valuable' and other people do not say it of me,
I shall be alone, there is no comfort there.
No, it is not comforting but it is valuable,
And if everybody says it in the end
It will be comforting. And for the panther too,
If everybody says he is valuable
It will be comforting for him.

Hymn to the Seal

To the tune: 'Soldiers of Christ arise!'
Hymns Ancient and Modern

Creature of God, thy coat
That lies all black and fine
I do admire, as on a sunny
Rock to see thee climb.

When thou wast young thy coat
Was pale with spots upon it,
But now in single black it lies
And thou, Seal, liest on it.

What bliss abounds to view
God's creatures in their prime
Climb in full coat upon a rock
To breathe and to recline.

Lord Say-and-Seal

Lord Say-and-Seal, Lord Say-and-Seal
Why not for once say and *reveal*
All the dark thoughts your words go over
To make a pretty bog-hole cover.

Yes, I know

That pale face stretches across the centuries
It is so subtle and yielding; yet innocent,
Her name is Lucretia Borgia.

Yes, I know. I knew her brother Cesare
Once. But only for a short time.

Voice from the Tomb (1)

Nightmare, after reading The Parable of the Talents.

Here lies a poet who would not write
His soul runs screaming through the night
Oh give me paper, give me pen,
And I will very soon begin.

Poor Soul, keep silent; in Death's clime
There's no pen, paper, notion,
And no Time.

Voice from the Tomb (2)

To the tune: 'From Greenland's icy mountains'.
Hymns Ancient and Modern

I trod a foreign path, dears,
The silence was extreme
And so it came about, dears,
That I fell into dream,

That I fell into dream, my dear,
And feelings beyond cause,
And tears without a reason
And so was lost.

Voice from the Tomb (3)

Such evidence I have of indifference
Were surely enough to break the coldest heart,
But this heart is not cold, it never has been cold,
It never, never, never has been cold.

Voice from the Tomb (4)

I died for lack of company
Did my dear friends not know?
Oh why would they not speak to me
Yet said they loved me so?

Voice from the Tomb (5)

A Soul earthbound by the grievance of never having been important.

You never heard of me, I dare
Say. Well, I'm here.

Pretty

Why is the word pretty so underrated?
In November the leaf is pretty when it falls
The stream grows deep in the woods after rain
And in the pretty pool the pike stalks

He stalks his prey, and this is pretty too,
The prey escapes with an underwater flash
But not for long, the great fish has him now
The pike is a fish who always has his prey

And this is pretty. The water rat is pretty
His paws are not webbed, he cannot shut his nostrils
As the otter can and the beaver, he is torn between
The land and water. Not 'torn', he does not mind.

The owl hunts in the evening and it is pretty
The lake water below him rustles with ice
There is frost coming from the ground, in the air mist
All this is pretty, it could not be prettier.

Yes, it could always be prettier, the eye abashes
It is becoming an eye that cannot see enough,
Out of the wood the eye climbs. This is prettier
A field in the evening, tilting up.

The field tilts to the sky. Though it is late
The sky is lighter than the hill field
All this looks easy but really it is extraordinary
Well, it is extraordinary to be so pretty.

And it is careless, and that is always pretty
This field, this owl, this pike, this pool are careless,
As Nature is always careless and indifferent
Who sees, who steps, means nothing, and this is pretty.

So a person can come along like a thief – pretty ! –
Stealing a look, pinching the sound and feel,
Lick the icicle broken from the bank
And still say nothing at all, only cry pretty.

Cry pretty, pretty, pretty and you'll be able
Very soon not even to cry pretty
And so be delivered entirely from humanity
This is prettiest of all, it is very pretty.

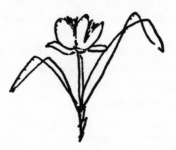

Animula, vagula, blandula

The Emperor Hadrian to his soul.

Little soul so sleek and smiling
Flesh's friend and guest also
Where departing will you wander
Growing paler now and languid
And not joking as you used to?

Friends of the River Trent

(*At their Annual Dinner*)

A dwindling body of ageing fish
Is all we can present
Because of water pollution
In the River Trent
Because of water pollution, my boys,
And a lack of concerted action,
These fish of what they used to be
Is only a measly fraction
A-swimming about most roomily
Where they shoved each other before,
Yet not beefing about being solitary
Or the sparseness of the fare.
Then three cheers for the ageing fish, my boys,
Content in polluted depths
To grub up enough food, my boys,
To carry 'em to a natural death,
And may we do the same, my boys,
And carry us to a natural death.

How Cruel is the Story of Eve

How cruel is the story of Eve
What responsibility
It has in history
For cruelty.

Touch, where the feeling is most vulnerable,
Unblameworthy – ah reckless – desiring children,
Touch there with a touch of pain?
Abominable.

Ah what cruelty,
In history
What misery.

Put up to barter
The tender feelings
Buy her a husband to rule her
Fool her to marry a master
She must or rue it
The Lord said it.

And man, poor man,
Is he fit to rule,
Pushed to it?
How can he carry it, the governance,
And not suffer for it
Insuffisance?
He must make woman lower then
So he can be higher then.

Oh what cruelty,
In history what misery.

Soon woman grows cunning
Masks her wisdom,
How otherwise will he
Bring food and shelter, kill enemies?
If he did not feel superior
It would be worse for her
And for the tender children
Worse for them.

Oh what cruelty,
In history what misery
Of falsity.

It is only a legend
You say? But what
Is the meaning of the legend
If not
To give blame to women most
And most punishment?
This is the meaning of a legend that colours
All human thought; it is not found among animals.

How cruel is the story of Eve,
What responsibility it has
In history
For misery.

Yet there is this to be said still:
Life would be over long ago
If men and women had not loved each other
Naturally, naturally,
Forgetting their mythology
They would have died of it else
Long ago, long ago,
And all would be emptiness now
And silence.

Oh dread Nature, for your purpose,
To have made them love so.

Mrs Arbuthnot

Mrs Arbuthnot was a poet
A poet of high degree,
But her talent left her;
Now she lives at home by the sea.

In the morning she washes up,
In the afternoon she sleeps,
Only in the evenings sometimes
For her lost talent she weeps,

Crying: I should write a poem,
Can I look a wave in the face
If I do not write a poem about a sea-wave,
Putting the words in place.

Mrs Arbuthnot has died,
She has gone to heaven,
She is one with the heavenly combers now
And need not write about them.

Cry: She is a heavenly comber,
She runs with a comb of fire,
Nobody writes or wishes to
Who is one with their desire.

Nodding

Tizdal my beautiful cat
Lies on the old rag mat
In front of the kitchen fire.
Outside the night is black.

The great fat cat
Lies with his paws under him
His whiskers twitch in a dream,
He is slumbering.

The clock on the mantelpiece
Ticks unevenly, tic toc, tic-toc,
Good heavens what is the matter
With the kitchen clock?

Outside an owl hunts,
Hee hee hee hee,
Hunting in the Old Park
From his snowy tree.
What on earth can he find in the park tonight,
It is so wintry?

Now the fire burns suddenly too hot
Tizdal gets up to move,
Why should such an animal
Provoke our love?

The twigs from the elder bush
Are tapping on the window pane
As the wind sets them tapping,
Now the tapping begins again.

One laughs on a night like this
In a room half firelight half dark

With a great lump of a cat
Moving on the hearth,
And the twigs tapping quick,
And the owl in an absolute fit
One laughs supposing creation
Pays for its long plodding
Simply by coming to this –
Cat, night, fire – and a girl nodding.

Some Are Born

Some are born to peace and joy
And some are born to sorrow
But only for a day as we
Shall not be here tomorrow.

How do you see?

How do you see the Holy Spirit of God?
I see him as the holy spirit of good,
But I do not think we should talk about spirits, I think
We should call good, good.

But it is a beautiful idea, is it not?
And productive of good?

Yes, that is the problem, it is productive of good,
As Christianity now is productive of good,
So that a person who does not believe the Christian faith
Feels he must keep silent, in case good suffers,
In case what good there is in the world diminishes.

But must we allow good to be hitched to a lie,
A beautiful cruel lie, a beautiful fairy story,
A beautiful idea, made up in a loving moment?

Yes, it is a beautiful idea, one of the most
Beautiful ideas Christianity has ever had,
This idea of the Spirit of God, the Holy Ghost,
My heart goes out to this beautiful Holy Ghost,
He is so beautifully inhuman, he is like the fresh air.
They represent him as a bird, I dislike that,
A bird is parochial to our world, rooted as we are
In pain and cruelty. Better the fresh air.

But before we take a Christian idea to alter it
We should look what the idea is, we should read in their books
Of holy instruction what the Christians say. What do they say
Of the beautiful Holy Ghost? They say

That the beautiful Holy Ghost brooded on chaos
And chaos gave birth to form. As this we cannot know

It can only be beautiful if told as a fairy story,
Told as a fact it is harmful, for it is not a fact.

But it is a beautiful fairy story. I feel so much
The pleasure of the bird on the dark and powerful waters,
And here I like to think of him as a bird, I like to feel
The masterful bird's great pleasure in his breast
Touching the water. Like! Like! What else do they say?

Oh I know we must put away the beautiful fairy stories
And learn to be good in a dull way without enchantment,
Yes, we must. What else do they say? They say

That the beautiful Holy Spirit burning intensely,
Alight as never was anything in this world alight,
Inspired the scriptures. But they are wrong,
Often the scriptures are wrong. For I see the Pope
Has forbidden the verse in Mark ever to be discussed again
And I see a doctor of Catholic divinity saying
That some verses in the New Testament are pious forgeries
Interpolated by eager clerks avid for good.

Ah good, what is good, is it good
To leave in scripture the spurious verses and not print
A footnote to say they are spurious, an erratum slip?

And the penal sentences of Christ: He that believeth
And is baptized shall be saved, he that believeth not
Shall be damned. Depart from me ye cursed into everlasting
    fire
Prepared for the devil and his angels. And then
Saddest of all the words in scripture, the words,
They went away into everlasting punishment. Is this good?

Yes, nowadays certainly it is very necessary before we take
The ideas of Christianity, the words of our Lord,
To make them good, when often they are not very good,
To see what the ideas are and the words; to look at them.

Does the beautiful Holy Ghost endorse the doctrine of eternal
    hell?
Love cruelty, enjoin the sweet comforts of religion?
Oh yes, Christianity, yes, he must do this
For he is your God, and in your books

You say he informs, gives form, gives life, instructs.
Instructs, that is the bitterest part. For what does he instruct
As to the dreadful bargain, that God would take and offer
The death of the Son to buy our faults away,
The faults of the faulty creatures of the Trinity?
Oh Christianity, instructed by the Holy Ghost,
What do you mean? As to Christ, what do you mean?

It was a child of Europe who cried this cry,
Oh Holy Ghost what do you mean as to Christ?
I heard him cry. Ah me, the poor child,
Tearing away his heart to be good
Without enchantment. I heard him cry:

Oh Christianity, Christianity,
Why do you not answer our difficulties?
If He was God He was not like us
He could not lose.

Can Perfection be less than perfection?
Can the creator of the Devil be bested by him?
What can the temptation to possess the earth have meant to
    Him
Who made and possessed it? What do you mean?

And Sin, how could He take our sins upon Him? What does
    it mean?

To take sin upon one is not the same
As to have sin inside one and feel guilty.

It is horrible to feel guilty,
We feel guilty because we are.
Was He horrible? Did He feel guilty?

You say He was born humble – but He was not,
He was born God –

Taking our nature upon Him. But then you say
He was perfect Man. Do you mean
Perfectly Man, meaning wholly? Or Man without sin? Ah
Perfect Man without sin is not what we are.

Do you mean He did not know that He was God,
Did not know He was the Second Person of the Trinity?
(Oh if He knew this and was,
It was a source of strength for Him we do not have)
But this theology of emptying you preach sometimes –
That He emptied Himself of knowing He was God – seems
A theology of false appearances
To mock your facts, as He was God whether He knew it or
    not.

Oh what do you mean, what do you mean?
You never answer our difficulties.

You say, Christiantity, you say
That the Trinity is unchanging from eternity,
But then you say
At the incarnation He took
Our Manhood into the Godhead
That did not have it before,
So it must have altered it,
Having it.

Oh what do you mean, what do you mean?
You never answer our questions.

So I heard the child of Europe cry,
Tearing his heart away
To be good without enchantment,
Going away bleeding.

Oh how sad it is to give up the Holy Ghost
He is so beautiful, but not when you look close,
And the consolations of religion are so beautiful,
But not when you look close.
Is it beautiful, for instance, is it productive of good
That the Roman Catholic hierarchy should be endlessly
    discussing at this moment
Their shifty theology of birth control, the Vatican

Claiming the inspiration of the Holy Spirit? No, it is not good,
Or productive of good. It is productive
Of contempt and disgust. Yet
On the whole Christianity I suppose is kinder than it was,
Helped to it, I fear, by the power of the Civil Arm.

Oh Christianity, Christianity,
That has grown kinder now, as in the political world
The colonial system grows kinder before it vanishes, are you
    vanishing?
Is it not time for you to vanish?

I do not think we shall be able to bear much longer the
    dishonesty
Of clinging for comfort to beliefs we do not believe in,
For comfort, and to be comfortably free of the fear
Of diminishing good, as if truth were a convenience.
I think if we do not learn quickly, and learn to teach children,
To be good without enchantment, without the help
Of beautiful painted fairy stories pretending to be true,
Then I think it will be too much for us, the dishonesty,
And, armed as we are now, we shall kill everybody,
It will be too much for us, we shall kill everybody.

A Soldier Dear to Us

It was the War
I was a child
They came from the trenches
To our suburb mild.

Our suburb then was more a country place
They came to our house for release.

In the convalescent Army hospital
That was once a great house and landed estate
Lay Basil, wounded on the Somme,
But his pain was not now so great

That he could not be fetched in a bath-chair
Or hobble on crutches to find in our house there
My mother and aunt, his friends on leave, myself (I was
    twelve)
And a hearth rug to lie down in front of the fire on and rest
    himself.

It was a November golden and wet
As there had been little wind that year and the leaves were yet
Yellow on the great trees, on the oak trees and elms
Of our beautiful suburb, as it was then.

When Basil woke up he liked to talk and laugh
He was a sweet-tempered laughing man, he said:
'My dear, listen to this' then he read
From The Church Times, how angry the Bishop was because
Of the Reserved Sacrament in the church
Of St Alban's, Holborn. 'Now, my dear' he said, 'for a treat
Next Sunday I will take you to All Saints, Margaret Street;
     only
You will have to sit on the ladies' side, though you are not yet
     one really.'

Basil never spoke of the trenches, but I
Saw them always, saw the mud, heard the guns, saw the
     duckboards,
Saw the men and the horses slipping in the great mud, saw
The rain falling and never stop, saw the gaunt
Trees and the rusty frame
Of the abandoned gun carriages. Because it was the same
As the poem 'Childe Roland to the Dark Tower Came'
I was reading at school.

Basil and Tommy and Joey Porteous who came to our house
Were too brave even to ask *themselves* if there was any hope
So I laughed as they laughed, as they laughed when Basil said:
What will Ronny do now (it was Ronny Knox) will he pope?

And later, when he had poped, Tommy gave me his book for
     a present,
'The Spiritual Aeneid' and I read of the great torment
Ronny had had to decide, Which way, this or that?
But I thought Basil and Tommy and Joey Porteous were
     more brave than that.

Coming to our house
Were the brave ones. And I could not look at them,
For my strong feelings, except
Slantingly, from the hearth rug, look at them.

Oh Basil, Basil, you had such a merry heart
But you taught me a secret you did not perhaps mean to impart,
That one must speak lightly, and use fair names like the ladies
They used to call
The Eumenides.

Oh Basil
I was a child at school,
My school lessons coloured
My thoughts of you.

Envoi

Tommy and Joey Porteous were killed in France. Now
    fifty years later
Basil has died of the shots he got in the shell crater
The shrapnel has worked round at last to his merry heart,
    I write this
For a memorial of the soldier dear to us he was.

Angel Boley

There was a wicked woman called Malady Festing
Who lived with her son-in-law, Hark Boley,
And her daughter Angel,
In a house on the high moorlands
Of the West Riding of Yorkshire
In the middle of the last century.

One day Angel
Overheard her mother, Malady, talking to Hark, her husband.
Hark, said Malady, it is time
To take another couple of children
Into our kitchen.
Hark laughed, for he too was wicked and he knew
For what purpose the little children
Were required.

But Angel, who was not happy and so
Lived out her life in a dream of absentmindedness,
In order not to be too much aware
Of her horrible relatives, and what it was
That happened every now and then
In the kitchen; and why the children who came
Were never seen again, this time
When she heard what her husband and mother said,
Came out of her absentmindedness and paid attention.
I know now, she said, and all the time I have known
What I did not want to know, that they kill all children
They lure to this house; and that is why, when I pass in the
        village,
The people look askance at me, and they whisper –
But not so that I cannot hear –

132

There goes the daughter of Mother Lure. And the stranger
   says:
Who is Mother Lure? And they answer: Mrs Festing and they
   make the sign
That is to protect them from evil. Selfish wretches, said Angel,
They do not mind about the children, that evil is not kept
   from *them*.
Angel wandered into the woods and she said: No more
   children
Are going to be murdered, and before they are murdered,
   tormented
And corrupted; no more children are going to be the victims
Of Mother Lure and my husband, Hark. Dark was the look
   then
On Angel's face, and she said: I am the Angel of Death.

Mrs Festing and Boley
Always left the cooking to Angel, they despised Angel but
    Angel
Could cook, and that they thought was all she was fit for,
To cook and keep house. And they realized
It was far from being to their disadvantage that Angel was,
As they thought, half-witted, and never knew
Or wanted to know, what was going on around her.

As soon as Angel
Said to herself: I am the Angel of Death
She became at once very practical and went out into the
    woods and fields
And gathered some A. Phalloides, commonly called the
    'white' or deadly
Amanita, a mushroom of high toxicity. These poisonous fungi
She put into a soup, and this soup she gave
To Hark, and her mother, Malady, for supper, so that they
    died.

Angel then went to the police and said:
I have done evil, but I have saved many children.

The Judge said: Why did you not tell the police
That children were being destroyed? There was no proof,
    said Angel,
Because there were no bodies. I never could find out
What they did with the children after they had killed them.

So then the police searched hard, the wells, the rivers and
    the woodlands,
But never could they find out where
The children lay. Nor had the parents of the children
At any time done anything but weep. For they thought their
    children

Had been bewitched and done away with, and that
If they told their fears of Mother Lure and her wickedness

To the police, they would not believe them, and more
    children than ever
Would disappear.

From then onwards in the trial, Angel spoke
No word more, except to say: I am the Angel of Death.
So they put her in a lunatic asylum, and soon she died
Of an outbreak of typhoid fever. The people of the village
Now loved Angel, because she had delivered them from the
    fear

Of Mother Lure and Hark Boley, and had saved their
Little children from being tormented and slain by these
    wicked people.
So they wrote on her tombstone: 'She did evil that good
Might come'. But the Vicar said it was better not to put this
    but
Just her name and age, which was sixteen.
So he had the words
The villagers had written taken off the tombstone.
    But the next day
The words were again on the tombstone;
    so again the Vicar had them
Removed. And this time a watch was set
    on the grave,
A police constable and the village sexton watched
    there that night.

And no man came again to write on the tombstone
The forbidden words. Yet when morning came,
Again the words were on the tombstone.
So the Vicar said: It is the hand of the Lord.

And now in that graveyard, at that grave's head beneath
    the yew trees,
Still stands today the tombstone of Angel, with the words
    writ on it:
'She did evil that good might come'. May God be merciful.

Cock-a-Doo

I love to hear the cock crow in
The middle of the day
It is an eerie sound in
The middle of the day
Sometimes it is a very hot day
Heavy for coming thunder
And the grass I tread on is dusty
And burnt yellow. Away
Over the river Bean which naturally
(It having been hot now for so long)
Runs shallow, stand up
The great yellow cornfields, but
Walking closely by the farm track
Not lifting my head, but foot by
Foot slowly, tired after a long
Walk, I see only the blue
And gray of the flint path, and
Each one of the particles of
Yellow dust on it. And this
Seeing, because of tiredness, becomes
A transfixion of seeing, more sharp
Than mirages are. Now comes the cry
Of the cock at midday
An eerie sound – cock-a-doooo – it
Sharpens a second time
The transfixion. If there were
A third sharpener
Coming this hot day with a butcher's edge
It would spell death.

Nor We of Her to Him

He said no word of her to us
Nor we of her to him,
But oh it saddened us to see
How wan he grew and thin.
We said: She eats him day and night
And draws the blood from him,
We did not know but said we thought
This was why he grew thin.

One day we called and rang the bell,
No answer came within,
We said: She must have took him off
To the forest old and grim,
It has fell out, we said, that she
Eats him in forest grim,
And how can we help him being eaten
Up in forests grim?

It is a restless time we spend,
We have no help for him,
We walk about and go to bed,
It is no help to him.
Sometimes we shake our heads and say
It might have better been
If he had spoke to us of her
Or we of her to him.
Which makes us feel helpful, until
The silence comes again.

The Word

My heart leaps up with streams of joy,
My lips tell of drouth;
Why should my heart be full of joy
And not my mouth?

I fear the Word, to speak or write it down,
I fear all that is brought to birth and born;
This fear has turned my joy into a frown.

Oh grateful colours, bright looks!

The grass is green
The tulip is red
A ginger cat walks over
The pink almond petals on the flower bed.
Enough has been said to show
It is life we are talking about. Oh
Grateful colours, bright looks! Well, to go
On. Fabricated things too – front doors and gates,
Bricks, slates, paving stones – are coloured
And as it has been raining and is sunny now
They shine. Only that puddle
Which, reflecting the height of the sky
Quite gives one a feeling of vertigo, shows
No colour, is a negative. Men!
Seize colours quick, heap them up while you can.
But perhaps it is a false tale that says
The landscape of the dead
Is colourless.

O Pug!

To the Brownes' pug dog, on my lap, in their car,
coming home from Norfolk.

O Pug, some people do not like you,
But I like you,
Some people say you do not breathe, you snore,
I don't mind,
One person says he is always conscious of your behind,
Is that your fault?

Your own people love you,
All the people in the family that owns you
Love you: Good pug, they cry, Happy pug,
Pug-come-for-a-walk.

You are an old dog now
And in all your life
You have never had cause for a moment's anxiety,
Yet,
In those great eyes of yours,
Those liquid and protuberant orbs,
Lies the shadow of immense insecurity. There
Panic walks.

Yes, yes, I know,
When your mistress is with you,
When your master
Takes you upon his lap,
Just then, for a moment,
Almost you are not frightened.

But at heart you are frightened, you always have been.

O Pug, obstinate old nervous breakdown,
In the midst of *so* much love,
And such comfort,
Still to feel unsafe and be afraid,

How one's heart goes out to you!

Archie and Tina

Archie and Tina
Where are you now,
Playmates of my childhood,
Brother and sister?

When we stayed in the same place
With Archie and Tina
At the seaside,
We used

To paddle the samphire beds, fish
Crabs from the sea-pool, poke
The anemones, run,
Trailing the ribbon seaweed across the sand to the sea's edge
To throw it in as far as we could. We dug
White bones of dead animals from the sandhills, found
The jaw-bone of a fox with some teeth in it, a stoat's skull,
The hind leg of a hare.

Oh, if only; oh if only!

Archie and Tina
Had a dog called Bam. The silver-sand
Got in his long hair. He had
To be taken home.

Oh, if only . . . !

One day when the wind blew strong
Our dog, Boy, got earache. He had
To be taken home in a jersey.

Oh what pleasure, what pleasure!·

There never were so many poppies as there were then,
So much yellow corn, so many fine days,
Such sharp bright air, such seas.

Was it necessary that
Archie and Tina, Bam and Boy,
Should have been there too?
Yes, then it was. But to say now:

Where are you today
Archie and Tina,
Playmates of my childhood,
Brother and sister? Is no more than to say:

I remember
Such pleasure, so much pleasure.

141

The Galloping Cat

Oh I am a cat that likes to
Gallop about doing good
So
One day when I was
Galloping about doing good, I saw
A Figure in the path; I said:
Get off! (Be-
cause
I am a cat that likes to
Gallop about doing good)
But he did not move, instead
He raised his hand as if
To land me a cuff
So I made to dodge so as to
Prevent him bringing it orf,
Un-for-tune-ately I slid
On a banana skin
Some Ass had left instead
Of putting in the bin. So
His hand caught me on the cheek
I tried
To lay his arm open from wrist to elbow
With my sharp teeth
Because I am
A cat that likes to gallop about doing good.
Would you believe it?
He wasn't there
My teeth met nothing but air,
But a Voice said: Poor cat,
(Meaning me) and a soft stroke
Came on me head
Since when
I have been bald.
I regard myself as

A martyr to doing good.
Also I heard a swoosh
As of wings, and saw
A halo shining at the height of
Mrs Gubbins's backyard fence,
So I thought: What's the good
Of galloping about doing good
When angels stand in the path
And do not do as they should
Such as having an arm to be bitten off
All the same I
Intend to go on being
A cat that likes to
Gallop about doing good
So
Now with my bald head I go,
Chopping the untidy flowers down, to
        and fro,
An' scooping up the grass to show
Underneath
The cinder path of wrath
Ha ha ha ha, ho,
Angels aren't the only ones who do
        not know
What's what and that
Galloping about doing good
Is a full-time job
That needs
An experienced eye of earthly
Sharpness, worth I dare say
(If you'll forgive a personal note)
A good deal more
Than all that skyey stuff
Of angels that make so bold as
To pity a cat like me that
Gallops about doing good.

Black March

I have a friend
At the end
Of the world.
His name is a breath

Of fresh air.
He is dressed in
Grey chiffon. At least
I think it is chiffon.
It has a
Peculiar look, like smoke.

It wraps him round
It blows out of place
It conceals him
I have not seen his face.

But I have seen his eyes, they are
As pretty and bright
As raindrops on black twigs
In March, and heard him say:

I am a breath
Of fresh air for you, a change
By and by.

Black March I call him
Because of his eyes
Being like March raindrops
On black twigs.

(Such a pretty time when the sky
Behind black twigs can be seen
Stretched out in one
Uninterrupted
Cambridge blue as cold as snow.)

But this friend
Whatever new names I give him
Is an old friend. He says:

Whatever names you give me
I am
A breath of fresh air,
A change for you.

The Sea-widow

How fares it with you, Mrs Cooper my bride?
Long are the years since you lay by my side.
Do you wish I was back? Do you speak of me dearest?
I wish you were back for me to hold nearest.
Who then lies nearer, Mrs Cooper my bride?
A black man comes in with the evening tide.
What is his name? Tell me! How does he dare?
He comes uninvited. His name is Despair.

Come, Death (2)

I feel ill. What can the matter be?
I'd ask God to have pity on me,
But I turn to the one I know, and say:
Come, Death, and carry me away.

Ah me, sweet Death, you are the only god
Who comes as a servant when he is called, you know,
Listen then to this sound I make, it is sharp,
Come Death. Do not be slow.

Index of Titles and First Lines

148

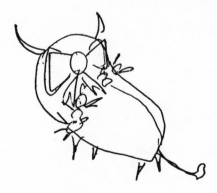